36

DISASTER

RESPONSE

and Planning for Libraries

Second Edition

MIRIAM B. KAHN

American Library Association
Chicago
2003

While extensive effort has gone into ensuring the reliability of information appearing in this book, the publisher makes no warranty, express or implied, on the accuracy or reliability of the information, and does not assume and hereby disclaims any liability to any person for any loss or damage caused by errors or omissions in this publication.

Composition by the dotted i in Goudy and Korinna using QuarkXPress 4.1 on a Macintosh platform

Printed on 50-pound white offset, a pH-neutral stock, and bound in 10-point cover stock by McNaughton & Gunn

The paper used in this publication meets the minimum requirements of American National Standard for Information Sciences—Permanence of Paper for Printed Library Materials, ANSI Z39.48-1992. ∞

Library of Congress Cataloging-in-Publication Data

Kahn, Miriam (Miriam B.)
   Disaster response and planning for libraries / Miriam B. Kahn. — 2nd ed.
      p.   cm.
   Includes bibliographical references and index.
   ISBN 0-8389-0837-3
   1. Libraries—Safety measures.   2. Library materials—Conservation and restoration.   3. Libraries—Safety measures—Planning.   4. Library materials—Conservation and restoration—Planning.   I. Title.
   Z679.7 .K38 2002
   025.8′2—dc21   2002008968

Printed in the United States of America

07 06 05 04 03   5 4 3 2 1

To those who lost their lives on September 11, 2001.

May we never forget.

And to those who responded using their well-tested plans.

Contents

Section 3 ■ Prevention

Section 4 ■ Planning

Section 5 ■ Response and Recovery Procedures

Appendixes

A ■ Checklists and Forms

Preface

In the aftermath of September 11, 2001, disaster response and all its related fields are more visible and seem more important to all of us. Heightened awareness of security issues, contingency plans, disaster response plans, and many other buzz words are present in the news and professional literature of almost every industry. In the wake of the attacks, the revision of this book was very timely. Even so, the primary focus of this publication is still damage to the tangible collections of libraries, archives, and historical societies. In the light of past events, library disaster response plans must continue to be integrated into disaster response plans of larger institutions and infrastructures, such as universities, museums, cities, counties, and states. September 11, 2001, has shown that preparing for small disasters is just as important as planning for the worst, or the unforeseen. Planning for disaster is an attempt to minimize the loss of information to clientele and decrease loss of access to and closure of collections. Without planning, the chances of survival of a business, information center, library, archives, or museum are next to impossible. Some planning will ensure part or all of the institution will survive to rebuild itself in a new and stronger manner.

Disasters, emergencies, and crises can occur in many forms:

Physical: fire, water, tornado, loss of power and phones, destruction of building or the collection, etc.

Personnel: loss of a key employee, employee dishonesty, sabotage, mental imbalance, etc.

While this publication addresses only physical disasters, you must keep in mind that many other events can be disastrous to your institution. These include bomb scares or major thefts.

This publication has been designed for use in libraries, archives, and historical societies to help respond to and recover from disasters and to assist in the design of disaster response plans. The materials are designed so that you can adapt the plan and procedures to your institution's needs.

Copies of the library's disaster response plan and computer backup tapes should be stored off-site at homes, record storage centers, or banks in case the library building is inaccessible. Keep at least one hard copy of the plan in each department and building. Update the plan whenever there are changes in personnel, hardware and software, and in the physical layout of the library/archives.

The plans and procedures in this publication are designed to be generic for library-type organizations. Placing this book on the shelf without taking the time to modify its procedures to your institution's needs means that you did not create a disaster response plan for your own organization. However, in the worst-case scenario, there are sections designed to be used as situations warrant. Moreover, designing and completing any plan does not guarantee that your institution will survive a disaster. It is merely one step in considering all the risks and preventing them. Planning for disasters will accomplish two things: increase the chances for you and your library to survive a disaster and decrease the impact afterward.

For additional information about disaster response planning, see the list of articles and publications listed in the bibliography at the end of this book.

Acknowledgments

Thanks for this second edition go to Clark Searle, who helped me work through the topics of mold and insurance and the issues of responsible record keeping during the response and recovery phases. Julie Callahan, thanks for helping me think through the librarian and archivist issues. Kirk Lively provided information on current disaster response companies and their specialized services. To my colleagues, Nancy Birk, Karen Benedict, and Marge Haberman go many thanks for listening to my new ideas and helping me form them into coherent concepts. Thanks to my editor Marlene Chamberlain for her encouragement during the slow and difficult spots. And, as always, thanks to my family for their support. The ideas and techniques in this book are the result of my experiences, feedback from the first edition, and from my workshops. Any errors and omissions are mine alone.

Introduction

Arrangement and Purpose

This publication is divided into five sections, two appendixes, and a bibliography—one section for each of the four phases of disaster response planning. The fifth section contains responses and procedures for stabilization and basic treatment of some collections, once the recovery process is in full swing. The first appendix includes checklists and forms that go with the different sections of the planning and prevention phases, and the second appendix lists different organizations, companies, and suppliers of disaster response services, consultation, and assistance. Five short case studies describe real-life library disasters, what happened, how they were dealt with, and what the outcomes were. A current bibliography is appended to this work for consultation and for in-depth information about some of the more complex issues.

This work provides practical, down-to-earth information and advice for dealing with disasters and planning for their eventual occurrence. There are quite a number of books in the field of disaster response and preparedness that cover theories of planning and of recovering print and non-print materials. Some ideas from those books are included, but the theory contained within is minimal and will mainly be found in the fifth section of this book.

As the focus is practicality, this publication begins with the most important aspect of a disaster response plan, "Response." This section comes first, just in case a reader needs to implement a response before there is an opportunity to put an actual plan together. The first section contains information on small jobs and how to handle them in-house with the institution's own staff and suggestions for hiring out the labor and supervising staff—all with an emphasis on the need to get back to normal as soon as possible.

Computers now play a truly integrated part in libraries, archives, and information centers. Our catalogs, circulation systems, and even collections and finding aids are located on these computers. So we must create disaster response plans for recovery of lost data, and resumption of online services and systems. These plans are usually called "contingency plans" and focus on restoring the programs and data carefully backed up every hour, day, or week. The specifics of planning for recovery of computer systems go beyond the scope of this publication. But I would be remiss to ignore the computers, so basic information and references about where the computer disaster response plan should be added or inserted will be included throughout. Some publications on the subject will be found in the bibliography.

The second section is "Recovery; or, Resumption of Normal Operations," which discusses the resumption of services and operations. It includes guidelines for what to do when the institution is no longer in disaster mode, including evaluating the effectiveness of the plan and modifying it as needed with additional staff training in the weak spots.

For the sake of simplicity, this book deals with response and recovery separately. However, as Camila Alire points out in her book, *Library Disaster Planning and Recovery Handbook*, ". . . the reality is that both activities (disaster response and recovery) can be operating at the same time."[1]

"Prevention," the third section, is closely tied in with "Planning." Prevention can stand alone and be accomplished without a formal disaster response plan.

"Planning," the fourth section, lists all responsibilities suggested for the team members; prioritizes the order of recovering damaged collections; and provides suggestions for staff training. This section is rounded out with information on how to plan for loss of computer services.

The fifth section, "Response and Recovery Procedures," includes information on handling, packing, drying, and cleaning print and non-print, paper and non-paper materials. There is information about dealing with mold and what effects ozone has on collections. Some of this section is taken from information collected by the author and distributed at seminars for libraries, archives, historical societies, and disaster response companies.

Of the two appendixes, the first, "Checklists and Forms," contains checklists and forms for use during all the phases of disaster response planning. They are fairly generic and so should be adapted for use at your institution. The second appendix, "Associations, Organizations, and Companies," contains a selected list of organizations, companies, and suppliers who can and will assist during disaster response, recovery, and planning. Not every organization or company is listed, mostly the large or national ones. Add your local contacts to make this plan your own.

The bibliography is divided into three parts. The first is a 10-item bibliography with books that contain the basics of planning and response. The second part lists publications arranged by topic and is designed to assist with specialized planning and recovery needs. The third part is a general bibliography containing additional readings that cross topic lines. The books, articles, and journals included in the bibliography are only some that are available in this flourishing field. Some citations refer to other bibliographies. Use the citations to educate the disaster response team and staff members of your institution.

Why Write a Disaster Response Plan?

More and more, disaster response and prevention are essential for the continuation of library business, be it serving patrons in the archives or library online services or providing staff with computers and other necessary equipment. With the proliferation of computers and our dependence upon data and online services, downtime or any lack of continuity is detrimental to quality service. So what is to be done? First, thinking about disasters, or "the worst," is the best first line of defense and prevention. If nothing ever went wrong, then disaster plans would be a waste of time. Sadly, this is not the case. Every day we read about floods, mold infections, and fires that cause irreparable harm to library and archival collections. Even a slowdown of service, as occurred in the federal government in 1995, has untold repercussions in quality of service and the ability to provide information in a timely manner.

In the aftermath of the destruction of the World Trade Center on September 11, 2001, financial institutions immediately activated the contingency plans for their computer systems. Through careful planning and testing, mandated by the federal government, they were able to restore operations quickly. Those businesses that did not have plans or data backed up in remote locations struggled to get their operations up and running. In some cases, all documents and data were lost forever.

While dealing with the enormity of the human tragedy, disaster response teams must plan effectively for the worst. After each disaster, the library and archives community learns the importance of foresight and planning for the loss of collections and data. (See the case study at the end of section 5.)

What Is a Disaster Response Plan and Why Is It Important?

Disaster response is the procedures and processes whereby a team of trained individuals responds to a disaster and determines how to best recover the damaged materials so that "business as usual" can resume as quickly as possible. It is best if the response and recovery procedures are worked out ahead of time. This will enable the disaster response team to implement response and recovery procedures as quickly as possible based upon well-thought-out priorities and techniques. During the disaster response phase of the operation, volunteers and outside consultants and contractors are often called in to assist with the recovery of damaged materials. It is important to consider the role of outside or volunteer assistance, where their services can best be used, how they can relieve physical and emotional stress from full-time staff, and how their services can be used to perform many of the labor-intensive procedures. A well-thought-out disaster response plan will decrease the amount of time it takes to implement disaster recovery procedures and should decrease the loss of materials and contents and increase the recovery rate.

In the *planning* phase, the disaster response team should be selected. Team members will be responsible for directing the activities during the response and recovery phases. The disaster response team should allocate responsibilities and assist with recovery prioritization decisions. The team should be involved with training for themselves and any staff and volunteers who will work on recovering the collections and facility from the disaster.

Preparation, or *preparedness*, is the phase in disaster response planning during which the disaster response team should survey the building and its collections for potential hazards and the identification of previous water leaks, etc. During this phase, the team should create simple floor plans to show where collections are located and what is in various rooms. The location of fire alarms, fire escapes and emergency doors, and fire extinguishers should also be identified. Disaster response planning and disaster prevention, or preparedness, are performed when all is sane and quiet, and decisions can be made in a rational, carefully considered manner.

On the flip side of the process, disaster response and recovery must be performed when there is chaos and when conflicting demands for restoring services, collections, and the facility are placed upon the disaster response team and the director. The response phase concentrates upon doing just that, responding to the news that a "disaster" has occurred and assembling the appropriate staff, outside assistance, and supplies to begin recovering the collection and the facility. The *recovery* phase concentrates on restoring the collection to a usable form and services to "normal" in a timely, efficient, and cost-effective manner.

Taken as a whole, a disaster response plan is essential to the continuation of the institution, retention of patrons, and fast and efficient resumption of services to patrons and staff.

Disaster Response Planning in a Nutshell

Consider the types of disasters most likely to happen or the crises that occur on a regular basis and plan for these, while keeping in mind disasters that might destroy the entire building or collection.

When planning for disasters, consider what services would be most affected by loss of access to the building and its collections. Is it access to the specialized collections, microfilm, and documents or the loss of payroll and financial information that keeps the institution funded? What other services will be disrupted? Other issues to consider and record:

- Who has the authority to order and pay for supplies and services that are needed?

- Who can make such decisions as calling the insurance company in to assess the loss and asking the disaster response firm and consultants to determine the scope of loss and the amount of work needed to "restore" the collection?

- Who has the authority to designate staff to "other duties as assigned," hire temporary staff, or rent space and equipment to work?

- Who is in charge of discussing the situation with the board of trustees or the director of the institution?

- Who will be the media spokesperson for the institution if there is no public information officer (PIO)?

- Who is responsible for declaring a disaster for the computer systems? Where will they set up temporary operation? What firm or individual stores the backup tapes? How quickly can the online system get back up and running?

These are just some of the many issues to be considered when designing the response portion of a plan. If you have ever been involved in a disaster, then you are aware that making decisions on the fly is not best for the library's collection or its personnel. Everyone is working under a high adrenaline level and may find it difficult to make educated, rational assessments of the situation and the condition of the remaining collections. Important materials could be damaged by being overlooked or discarded accidentally. Recovery decisions need to be prioritized ahead of time, during the planning process. Disaster response planning takes time but is well worth the effort.

What If the Disaster Happens Before You Have a Plan?

If you don't have a plan and a disaster occurs, take the following seven steps.

1. Gather together key staff in a quiet place, either in the building or near it.

2. Assess the scope of the damage and potential disruption of primary services and functions. Review affected collections for importance within the library's mission and in terms of the magnitude of damage from water or fire.

3. Contact colleagues outside of the institution for assistance and recommendations for consultants and disaster response/drying companies.

4. Assign staff to recovery responsibilities:

   - Performing physical work
   - Acting as liaison with administration and performing administrative work
   - Communicating with both internal and external organizations (with media and others outside of the institution)
   - Contacting your insurance agent. Ask about disaster response assistance and available funds.
   - Working with disaster response companies and consultants
   - Locating alternative work areas and supplies

5. Meet again with key staff to coordinate the recovery operation.

6. Begin the recovery operation, starting with primary priorities and services.

7. Start phasing in the return of primary services and functions.

Place a basic response plan with phone numbers in the front of your disaster response manual for easy reference and contact. Post the daytime numbers for the disaster response team at phones for a swift response.

Endnote

1. Camila Alire, *Library Disaster Planning and Recovery Handbook* (New York: Neal-Schuman, 2000), p. 12.

Response

isaster strikes! Suddenly everyone and everything goes crazy. Your adrenaline pumps, and the disaster response team has to *do something* about the disaster! Hopefully, this is the moment you have been working toward, making plans and trying to prevent additional damage to collections.

Response comes about in three phases:

1. Responding to notification of the disaster

2. Assessing the situation and damage

3. Beginning to rescue and recover collections

PHASE ONE
Responding to Notification of the Disaster

First, assemble the disaster response team. During the planning phase you should have selected a place to meet outside the building if the entire library or building was damaged; otherwise, meet in a conference room inside the building. If there is no disaster response team in place, gather together department heads, the preservation or rare books/special collections librarian, and the library/archives director.

The director should select a team leader from this group. Don't forget to notify the head of Information Systems. This department may have special needs for the implementation of their part of the disaster response plan.

Next, the disaster response team leader should brief the disaster response team about the situation. Review the responsibilities and call in additional staff if necessary. The disaster may be caused by water, fire (which will leave you with water afterward), or loss of power and phones. If it is the latter, implement procedures to provide services manually and contact the utility company. At this point, the computer disaster response team should activate their plan to operate from a remote location and provide assistance to check collections in and out using the backup circulation system, if any. If the power or phones will be out for an extended period of time, then determine how to provide those services from a remote location or by referral. The following response procedures pertain primarily to damage from fire and water:

- Close the building or the damaged area to the public.

5

- Shut the water off and find out if the other utilities are on or should be turned off.
- Start the response operation, and activate the basic internal communications policy.

PHASE TWO
Assessing the Situation and Damage

This next phase of the disaster response plan requires that the building or area be safe to enter.

First, the disaster response team needs to assess the damage. Walk through the damaged area to see what really happened. Make a list of the areas that require *pack out*, cleanup, or removal to storage. Check the damaged collection against the "Prioritization for Recovery Checklist." (Prioritization for recovery should have been determined during the planning phase; if not, call in the subject specialist or bibliographer to make up a basic prioritization list. Give him or her the prioritization criteria. See appendix A, number 4.)

In addition to the disaster response team, the Information Systems team should be called in to determine the extent of damage to the online public access catalog (OPAC), circulation systems, and website. Coordinate the use of personnel and resources during the phases of recovery of data and reintegration of systems. Be certain to continue to include the Information Systems' head of their disaster response team in all meetings.

Next, brief the director of the library/archives or the head of the institution about the situation. Activate the external communications plan. Decide if the building or area needs to remain closed, and if so, estimate for how long.

Finally, contact the appropriate outside assistance, consultants, and drying company. Call in additional staff to assist with the recovery operation. Assemble the necessary supplies to begin the cleanup.

PHASE THREE
Beginning to Rescue and Recover Collections

Talk with facilities maintenance staff, or with the disaster response/drying company if they will be performing this service, and have the standing water removed.

Start to pack out the water-damaged and smoke-damaged items for freezing or air drying. A good rule of thumb is: less than 500 volumes can be air dried locally if desired; less than 100 volumes should be treated in-house. If more than 500 volumes were damaged by water, send them to a freezer storage facility to await decisions and funds for vacuum freeze-drying.

Next, move the dry and undamaged items into storage or a temporary access area if a large portion of the area or building was damaged. This will prevent secondary damage from increased levels of moisture and relative humidity. If it is impractical to move the undamaged items to another location, then set up fans and drop the temperature in the damaged area. Air movement and decreased temperature will lower the chance for a mold outbreak.

Then, discard wet and irreparably damaged items and debris so they no longer contribute moisture to the building and other materials. This will decrease the chance for a mold outbreak.

Set up fans to move the air, adjust the HVAC (heating, ventilating, and air-conditioning) system to dry the air and stabilize the environment.

Now you are ready to concentrate on the recovery phase. This begins after the immediate crisis, actions, and emotions are under control. Recovery will be covered in section 2.

Remove all damaged computer equipment for cleaning, repair, and recertification. Move any undamaged computer equipment to a safe location, remote storage, or off-site operations center. Coordinate with Information Systems' disaster response.

Call for Outside Assistance

During the response phase, it is important to ask for outside assistance, even if the disaster response team thinks it can handle the situation alone. The only time you might not call for help is if the disaster is very isolated and has affected only a few volumes. Otherwise, you will want outside guidance and assistance for one or two days, until the situation is under control and the emotional stress has decreased.

It is important for the person or company providing assistance to be familiar with the collection and the institution's policies. The outside consultant or company is not emotionally tied to the collections and is therefore capable of presenting choices and options where the staff's emotions and attachment to materials may rule.

Consultants provide additional assistance by bringing in help from disaster response/drying companies and others who specialize in conservation of the unique, fragile, and non-print/non-paper items in the collections. A consultant, working in conjunction with the disaster response team leader, relieves the director of the archives or library of the day-to-day stress of dealing with cleaning up the disaster, possibly with the help of temporary laborers hired to do much of the non-skilled physical labor. If necessary, the consultant and the disaster response team member responsible for working with volunteers should work with the disaster response company, demonstrating how to move books and pack boxes for shipment. One or both should be the liaison between the company and the library/archives.

The director of the library/archives might wish to have the consultant prepare recommendations, bid specifications for specialized work, demonstrate procedures for cleanup and mold prevention and removal, and perhaps even write temporary policies for the institution. As a follow-up, ask the consultant to write recommendations for preventing future disasters.

Damage Assessment

First, take out the "Prioritization for Recovery Checklist" (p. 103) and see "Prioritization Categories" (p. 45) and review the *established* criteria as well as the collection policy and mission statement for the institution. *Do not change the criteria or prioritization at this time.* Decisions made under stress and with adrenaline, or when emotions are high, are not always rational and justifiable or based upon the or-

ganization's mission statement. If no decisions were made prior to the disaster, ask for outside assistance from a consultant familiar with your collections and selection policies.

Now, walk through the damaged areas carefully. Photograph or videotape the damage for the insurance adjuster. Checklists 5–9 for documenting damage assessment are located in appendix A pages 95–99. It is not always necessary for the adjuster to be present when you begin the response and recovery phases of disaster response. It is necessary that the insurance company be aware that the disaster occurred and that the disaster response team knows what can and cannot be done within the policy's terms.

While documenting the damage, check collections against your checklist or the prioritization categories. List what to do with specific parts of the collection.

Use copies of the floor plans to show what to work on and when. Indicate the wet items to be removed for packing and where the packing area will be. Indicate the dry collections, whether portions within the damaged areas will need to be moved, and to where.

Note the types of damage (water, soot, debris, etc.) to the different areas of the collection and the types of cleanup necessary when the recovery phase begins.

If there is structural damage to the building, such as a hole in the roof, broken windows, or holes in doors and walls, list the damage. Get security to protect the building from unauthorized persons. Have facilities maintenance staff board up the windows and doors. Have a company come in to cover the holes in the roof. Make certain the roof covering is secure enough to withstand the rain. It should have some type of drainage so that if there is rain or snow, the tarp does not fill with water and collapse into the building. Get damaged roof areas repaired right away. This area is a prime candidate for causing additional damage to the structural integrity of the building and an avenue for mold infections.

Determine if it is possible to segregate the damaged area from the rest of the building. If so, do that. Remember to close off the space between the suspended ceiling and the "true" ceiling. Begin activities to stabilize the environment in the remaining undamaged parts of the building.

Consult with the Information Systems disaster response team and add their input into the assessment phase.

Make a list of necessary supplies, equipment, and services. Have the disaster response team member responsible for this begin to work on requisitioning and collecting the items. If no disaster response team member is assigned to do this, designate an appropriate staff member and obtain the authorization to spend money from the director.

When the survey of the damaged building is complete, review the list of work to be performed, using checklists 10–13 found in appendix A, pages 100–101. Divide the damaged area up among staff for supervision of activities.

Begin recovery with the first category of priority for recovery. Start removal of standing water and debris. Remove the damaged items from the floor, then the shelves. When the first priority collections have been dealt with in that area of the building, move to the second priority.

Response to Different-Size Disasters

Small scale disasters usually require the disaster response team members, the department's staff, and facilities maintenance personnel. Collect supplies and equipment for cleaning up the disaster from in-house supplies. It will probably not be necessary to close the building to deal with a very small disaster, but consider closing the affected department until all is cleaned up.

Small Scale

Examples of small disasters include excessive condensation and dripping from the air-handling system or a sink or toilet that overflowed into the collection. The former is sometimes difficult to detect and may come to light when a mold infection is discovered.

Water leaks from sinks, pipe joints, and toilets should be shut off or stopped as soon as they are discovered, the water leak repaired, and the collection

and the area dried out. Watch for mold outbreaks afterward from water that was trapped in the walls, ceilings, or carpets. Monitor the relative humidity to confirm that the air-handling system is controlling the environment.

A small scale disaster usually involves less than 500 damaged items (several stacks or ranges of books) or an isolated area of the collection. Two to six people should be sufficient to deal with the disaster and stabilize the area. If the "small" disaster is large enough to require the assistance of most of the staff, close the building until the immediate response is well under way. Depending upon the amount of damage caused by a "small" disaster, operations and services should return to normal within two to eight hours. Response steps should include removing the water and packing up damaged items in the collection for freezing and vacuum freeze-drying if more than 500 items are wet or for air drying if fewer than 500 items are damaged.

Don't forget to let staff in the building and the institution know about the disaster and how it was handled. Remember to look at the disaster response plan afterward and determine how it helped with cleanup and recovery. Revise those sections of the plan that were deficient or lacking.

Large Scale or Wide Area

Large scale and wide-area disasters constitute the more catastrophic situations that occur in libraries, archives, and historical societies. They usually involve a large portion of the building or the institution as a whole. A large scale disaster involves at least 500 items in the collection. A wide-area disaster involves the entire institution, city, or county. Personnel to deal with the response and recovery aspects of the disaster includes the disaster response team members, all staff, facilities maintenance, security, and outside contractors (consultants or a disaster response/drying company or both).

Examples of large scale disasters are a leak in the roof or a major water-pipe break that soaks a large portion of the collection or goes unreported overnight so that there are four to six inches of standing water on the floor. Wide-area disasters are usually caused by nature, such as a hurricane, tornado, or flood, and involve an entire geographical area. However, there are wide-area man-made disasters, most recently the destruction of the World Trade Center in New York City and the damage to the Pentagon in Washington, D.C., caused by bombs and explosives. In this case, the area's infrastructure was damaged or destroyed, necessitating the temporary relocation of the library/archive or at least the public assistance and information operations of the institution. Disaster response plans and contingency plans were activated and staff reassigned pending assessment of the damage.

Both large scale and wide-area disasters necessitate closing the building or operations, for at least 24 to 48 hours or longer until the basic recovery operations are well under way and all the standing water and debris are removed. Damaged materials should be packed and moved to freezer storage or a vacuum freeze-drying company for drying and cleaning. Supplies and equipment necessary to perform the response and recovery operations will initially be drawn from in-house supplies, then obtained from the outside sources identified during the planning phase.

When the disaster occurs, activate the *communications* part of the plan. Let staff know where to report and which staff should report at what time. Keep the institution's administration informed of the situation. Notify vendors and suppliers of any changes in location or phone numbers, and let them know how to get in touch with the institution. Release information to the press as to the scope of the disaster, how long you plan to be closed, how to contact the institution, and if donations or assistance are needed. (Consult the communications part of the plan, in section 4, for details.) This information should also direct patrons and clients to alternative locations and services in the community.

When the response and recovery operation is under control, reopen the building. It might be necessary to keep the badly damaged areas closed. If so, determine how to get the undamaged materials to patrons while keeping them out of the area. After the water, dust, soot, and debris are removed and the collection is "safe" again, open up the area. It may take weeks or months to get the damaged portion of the collection back on the shelves. In the meantime, set up a routine for checking the dam-

aged areas for mold and any standing water. Monitor the relative humidity and temperature of the damaged areas to make certain the HVAC system is keeping the environment stable.

In the case of a wide-area disaster, where the building or surrounding areas are destroyed or untenable, the library, archive, or information center will need to relocate to another branch or location altogether. If the library is part of a branch system, another library will have to take on the additional burden, with staff distributed throughout the system. If the library stands alone, then a new location will have to be found. If the primary mission of the library is information retrieval and dissemination, as in a business library, then it should be possible to work from a remote location or from another business library for a short while, or even telecommute. Careful coordination with the Information Systems disaster response team is essential to get the information retrieval function of the library or archive back to normal.

As follow-up to the disaster, issue another press release informing the public that the situation is back to "normal," that operations and services have been restored, and what the residual damage is, if any. Contact vendors and suppliers and let them know the outcome of the disaster. Write about the disaster and its aftermath for professional publications. Discuss the disaster and its aftermath with staff, the disaster response team members, and outside contractors. Answer questions and evaluate the response plan for its strong and weak points. Modify the plan accordingly.

Dealing with the Media

Once response efforts are under way, it is important to let people know what happened and what is needed, if anything. The communications portion of the plan should be activated.

- Inform the staff as soon as the immediate disaster is discovered.
- Release information to the vendors and suppliers of products and services and to the media and the public at the same time.

- Press releases should be mailed, faxed, and e-mailed to suppliers of services and products, giving them the temporary location, phone and fax numbers, contact person, and hours.

- The designated spokesperson or public information officer for the institution should let the media and the public know what happened and what is being done to recover collections and resume services. If donations of time, supplies, collections, or money are desired, tell them what you want and who to contact. Include the temporary location, phone and fax numbers, contact person, and hours. If items in circulation are out, let the public know where to return them or if they should hold on to the materials.

- Distribute a press release to the local TV stations, radio stations, and newspaper. If there is a web page for the collections or institution, include temporary contact information on the page.

Remember, only *one person* should be designated to speak for the institution to avoid conflicting or negative accounts of the disaster.

Working with Contractors

In the planning phase, the library/archives staff will have met with consultants and disaster response/drying companies. When the disaster occurs, contact the outside contractors to come in to assist in response and recovery. Now you have to work with them.

Keep a few things in mind. The insurance adjuster has, or appears to have, a lot of control over whom to hire. Bids go out and the adjuster usually picks the lowest bid. Remember that the adjuster may not be familiar with the true costs to recover, dry, and clean the collection and the building. Have some cost ranges for recovery on hand to show the adjuster just what to expect in terms of a bill. If a contractor is predesignated in the response plan, this should work in your favor for permission from the insurance company to go ahead with recovery.

For the bid, especially if you don't have a predesignated contractor, provide written specifica-tions for the type of work to be done and the type of drying required. Hold the insurance adjuster and the contractor to these specifications. You should discuss the specifications for recovery with the adjuster. The institution has the right to specify a company in its plan and to specify particular treatments and drying techniques.

Select three acceptable disaster response/drying companies to bid on the work. Walk them through the building and discuss what is damaged, the priorities for recovery, and the drying technique required. Ask for an itemized bid.

When evaluating the bid, watch for hidden costs, such as shipping and packing and labor at the disaster response/drying company. Also ask for clarification of any vague breakdown in price. Require a "Not to Exceed" bid.

Once the contractor is hired, the disaster response team member designated as the liaison starts to work harder. Assign another staff member to alternate with the disaster response team member. Get together with the contractor to

- review the priorities for recovery and the "to do" list,

- walk through the damaged area again,

- schedule frequent, at least daily, meetings with the contractor,

- document all meetings, conversations, telephone calls, and e-mail messages,

- provide written instructions for all changes to bid and get prices before approval of changes, and

- approve all changes in writing.

Involve the director if additional expenditures of funds need to be made.

The disaster response team member should monitor what the contractor and his or her staff are doing, how they are handling the collection, and how they are cleaning the building and collection. Provide feedback for the contractor. The liaison is there to answer questions and make some additional prioritization decisions.

Watch the costs incurred by the contractor and the institution. Remember that every change to what was asked for in the "Request for Bid" increases the cost of recovery. Do not sign off on the work until it is done to your specifications.

Working with contractors is one phase of response and recovery where an independent consultant will be useful. You can ask the consultant to write the specifications and recommendations for the bid and to perform quality-control checks. Consultants can be asked to meet with the administrators, to explain processes and specifications to insurance agents, and to discuss the disaster and secondary ramifications with the staff. In some cases, the consultant may be asked to work in tandem with the disaster response team leader or as an alternate.

Conservation centers typically provide two types of services in disaster response: a consultant and conservation on specific items that require specialized treatments. If you have an independent consultant already working with the institution who is capable of handling preservation and disaster response issues, use that consultant. This person is already familiar with the collections, mission statements, and staff. If the institution has not worked with an independent consultant, then contact a local or regional conservation center to ask for either their preservation consultant to help for a few days or for a referral to an independent consultant.

As to individual items requiring specialized treatment, work with a local or regional conservation center to get a bid on stabilization and treatment. The items requiring this specialized treatment should be segregated from the mass-recovery effort early in the response phase. Such items should have been identified during the prioritization phase. Get the materials stabilized according to the conservator's instructions and placed in storage at the conservation center awaiting permission or funding to begin treatment. Money for conservation treatment may come from the insurance company or from a contingency fund, depending upon coverage and the type of work required. Be certain to ask when the center can begin treatment.

It is important to keep in mind that conservation centers traditionally treat specific items one-by-one and not en masse. They will not be able to handle the thousands or tens of thousands of items that are damaged during the disaster. Rely upon the conservation centers for specialized treatments, handling, and care.

Recovery Decisions and Priorities

If the decision is to dry and place water-damaged materials back on the shelf, the following are guidelines on how to handle these items. If collections are not wet, cover or move them to a dry location.

Paper

> Plain—attend to within 72 hours.
>
> Clay-coated (shiny) paper, including thermal-fax and self-carboned paper—remove from water and treat within 6 hours of exposure to water.

Microfilm/microfiche

> Attend to within 72 hours.
>
> Hang to dry or keep wet and send for reprocessing.

Motion picture film, post-1950 negatives, slides, and post-1950 photographs

> Attend to within 72 hours.
>
> Hang to dry or keep wet and freeze quickly.

Pre-1950 photographs and negatives

> Contact photograph conservator before treating or freezing.

CD-ROMs and optical discs

> Treat immediately.
>
> Dry and clean appropriately.

Magnetic tape

> Remove from water immediately.
>
> Dry and clean appropriately.

Computer tapes without backup copies

> Treat immediately.
>
> Identify format, computer type, and amount of space used on tapes.
>
> Send for drying and copying.

Diskettes without backup copies

> Treat immediately.
>
> Dry, clean, and recopy.

Hardware

> Dry, clean, and recertify.
>
> Keyboards—replace.
>
> Monitors—clean or replace depending upon value.
>
> Unique or obsolete hardware—upgrade or clean depending upon insurance.

Office equipment: fax, copier, etc.

> Dry, clean, and recertify.

Computers and Disaster Recovery

When systems crash or data are garbled, the information systems department or librarian is usually responsible for restoring computer services and getting data loaded from backup tapes.

Computer systems that sustain damage from water, dust, soot, fire, or construction are not automatically lost or irreparably damaged. Hardware can sustain water damage without many problems. For water damage, turn off and unplug the equipment and peripherals, open the covers or cases, remove the standing water, and dry out the components. Clean the computer components, and check with your insurance company or computer maintenance contractor about recertification of the hardware. Do not plug in the computers or peripherals until they are dried and cleaned.

Fire and construction activities will introduce a fine layer of dust, soot, or debris on every surface of the library, archives, or historical society. If you are aware that construction is taking place in the building, cover all computer equipment and peripherals to prevent damage. If the equipment becomes contaminated with dust, soot, or debris, unplug the components and vacuum out the debris. *Do not use water.* When the equipment is clean, plug it in and check that everything works properly.

If data, diskettes, and magnetic tape appear to be damaged, do not lose hope. Remove the diskettes and tapes that are lying in water. If there is water inside the tape cartridges, find out if there is a backup copy. If not, open them up and let the water drain out, copy the tape or diskette, then clean the drive.

Check the new tape or diskette for completeness of data and make certain it works before discarding the original. In some cases it is easier and more efficient to hire out the cleaning and copying of computer tapes and diskettes.

A separate disaster response plan for restoration of computer operations is imperative. The plan should stand alone. Be certain to indicate where the pieces of the disaster response plan for computers fit into the library's disaster response plan. During a large scale and wide-area disaster, integration of the priorities, computer, fiscal, and personnel, must be considered during the assessment phase. Communication between the two teams during the disaster response and recovery phases of the plan is essential. For basic plans, consult the publications listed in the computer section of the bibliography

Different Methods of Drying Wet Materials

Clay-coated paper will stick together and form a solid mass when wet. The substance that makes the paper shiny is called "clay," and it is essentially an adhesive that will stick to whatever it touches when wet. Clay-coated paper is found in many periodicals and books with reproductions of artworks and photographs. During the prioritization for recovery process (found in section 4, "Planning"), decide what will be done to water-damaged clay-coated paper.

Deep-freeze or blast freeze (that is, freeze quickly) soaked materials as soon as possible. This stabilizes the materials and prevents additional damage, inhibits mold, and prevents clay-coated papers from sticking together. Freezing is a delaying tactic until further evaluation of the materials can determine the best method of drying or whether to discard the items.

Vacuum thermal-drying and vacuum freeze-drying were both invented in the 1960s and are the most common methods for drying water-damaged materials.

The vacuum thermal-drying process starts with materials in a frozen state. A vacuum is introduced, and the air is heated to between 50° and 1000° Fahrenheit. As the vacuum is reduced, *the ice melts and the water becomes a vapor.* The freeze-and-thaw process may cockle or wrinkle the paper. The vacuum thermal-drying process can produce extreme warping due to the release of adhesives in the binding and under the cloth when exposed to heat; therefore, rebinding may be required. This process may be okay for loose papers and non-valuable materials. However, water-soluble inks may run, and clay-coated papers may stick together due to the extreme heat and moisture. Vacuum thermal-drying is not suitable for leather or vellum.

Vacuum freeze-drying also starts with frozen materials. A vacuum is introduced, but no heat is added, so the contents are dried at temperatures below 32° Fahrenheit. Ice is sublimated into vapor by passing from the frozen to a gaseous state. Therefore, papers do not become wet a second time. As a result, less rebinding is required. This process is good for coated papers if they are frozen within six hours of exposure to water. Vacuum freeze-drying may be suitable for leather or vellum and water-soluble inks. Consult a conservator first.

Air drying and dehumidification are the best treatments for materials that are slightly wet and that can be handled within a working day. Clay-coated papers should be frozen if you are not able to attend to them within six hours of exposure to water.

Air drying uses fans in combination with a decrease in temperature in the building. Books may be distorted when dry and require rebinding. Dehumidification uses dehumidifiers in a controlled space to dry the books. The bindings may be distorted afterward, requiring rebinding.

Photographic materials are best suited to air drying without freezing if it is possible to treat them immediately. Otherwise, freeze the photographs and negatives if you are unable to treat them within three working days. Then either thaw and air dry or vacuum freeze-dry, if there is no monetary value attached to the images. Be aware that vacuum freeze-drying may result in loss of the emulsion layer. Contact a conservator if you have questions about this process and its outcome.

Paper, books, and film-based materials can be vacuum freeze-dried with a minimum of distortion and loss. Magnetic tape can be vacuum freeze-dried but *should not be frozen*. Freezing makes magnetic tape brittle and can dry up the lubricants.

Remove soot, dirt, and mold after the drying process is complete.

Emotional Issues

During the response and recovery phases, along with adrenaline, emotions run high, and together they create stress, which expresses itself as both physical and mental stress. Sometimes the stress manifests itself in an inability to function, guilt complexes, and a decreased level of morale.

The emotions and adrenaline and the event itself combine to create guilt. This shows itself in staff working very long hours without sufficient breaks and striving toward superhuman efforts to do more than required. The guilt can manifest itself in physical work that may result in accidents from doing too much and being overtired. Some staff take disasters personally and think they are the *only ones* who can "set things straight."

In the case of a wide-area disaster, reactions may range from shock and disbelief to anger and guilt and numbness and grief to depression. Some ways to deal with this guilt complex are to require and enforce breaks and to divide the staff into several shifts. Hold meetings to remind staff that the disaster is not their fault and to praise the efforts of the disaster response team and staff members for their work and the results.

Mental stress will be most visible in the disaster response team and director of the library/archives. The mental stress comes from dealing with the overload of work to be done and the decisions to be made. Minimizing this stress is one of the main reasons for the plan and the prioritization for recovery being completed ahead of time.

Physical stress, along with an inability to function, is the way some people deal with disasters. One way to deal with this problem is to put the staff person to work physically to try to release the tension and emotions that are bottled up inside. If this does not relieve the stress, either assign the staff member work unrelated to the recovery efforts or send the person home for a day or two.

Decreased morale can be the result of a number of events, but it usually is present when the disaster is a repeat of the first or second disaster earlier in the year, or if the recovery efforts are going slowly and seem hopeless. Some ways to deal with decreased morale are to have the director of the library/archives or the head of the institution meet with the staff several times during the response and recovery phases of the disaster to provide updates on the situation. The director should praise the work and recognize the efforts made by all. If morale continues to decline or the recovery efforts continue for many days, schedule "off time" for the disaster response team and staff who are helping out, and arrange for food and drink during breaks. Don't forget that breaks and the opportunity to get away from the stress and the physical work will assist with boosting morale.

During a wide-area disaster, emotional issues and stress are compounded when staff members worry about their families and homes. They will be torn between taking care of personal problems and the guilt associated with helping out at work. Many will feel that personal crises take precedence over work.

The following methods help deal with this conflict:

- Increase reliance on staff living outside the disaster zone. Put these staff members into the key positions and rotate them with the disaster response team members.

- Increase the use of contractors and consultants. Select the contractors from outside the disaster area if possible. Even though there may be more start-up difficulties with contractors unfamiliar with the area, they should be able to draw from less-depleted resources.

- Provide time off for staff dealing with family and home crises. This is especially important if all staff live within the damaged area.

- Allow for flexibility in the rules of reporting to work on time and unscheduled absences to permit staff to deal with home and family issues.

- Make counseling available to all staff members. This counseling will serve two primary purposes: it allows staff to talk out the emotional issues and conflicts and provides assistance with crises at home.

The disaster response team leader and members should be aware of the increase in emotions and try to channel them toward the desired end of the recovery operation.

The response phase continues until the cleanup is well under way and administrators are beginning to think about resuming the full range of services and operations.

We plan for disasters with the intention of responding to them quickly and efficiently. The end result is not always what we hoped for—that is, the collection will be saved, intact, and the staff will take it all in stride. The larger and wider the disaster, the more everything and everyone within the institution are affected.

The following is the first of five case studies. Each presents a summary of what happened during and after a disaster and how cultural institutions dealt with the events and the results.

CASE STUDY ONE

Fire in City Archives, Linkoping, Sweden

Lars Bjordal, a paper conservator at Uppsala University Library, Sweden, was sent to Linkoping to help deal with conservation of paper documents after a fire. He sent this message to the Conservation Discussion List on October 3, 1996, where he describes the fire and its aftermath.[1]

On 21 September 1996, the City Library in Linkoping, Sweden, burned to the ground. With the fire went not only the library, but also the city archives that were located in the building. The reaction to the catastrophe showed, however, that people in general attach great importance to public libraries and archives, which warms the heart in this sad moment.

How is the situation now and how big was the damage? Three experts from Uppsala University Library went down to Linkoping: Per Cullhed, a book conservator; Lars Bjordal, a paper conservator; and the coordinator of the International Council on Archives working group on disaster planning, Ingmar Frojd. Lars Bjordal's impressions from the visit follow:

The fire started in one or two of the office rooms that were situated on the first floor in the main building. The rapid spreading of the fire indicates that it was set by someone using gasoline or something like that, and nothing points out that it was the result of a technical problem. About 30 minutes after the fire alarm was activated, the main building collapsed in an explosion from the fire gases. The fire brigade then concentrated their resources on saving the administration building next door, which they managed to do. Although there were more than 400 people in the building at the time the fire started, there were no injuries. The library staff tried to stop the fire, but after a few minutes they gave up and concentrated on getting all the people out of the building. They did brilliant work.

The books (ca. 200,000 vol.), the catalog, a special collection on literature from the county, archival material, old paintings, and much more were destroyed in the main building.

The older collections of books (ca. 250,000 vol.) and archival documents, etc., were saved! They were stored in the cellar of the main building. Although the cellar roof was strong enough to protect against the fire, there were huge cracks in some parts of it as a result of the high pressure from the collapsed building above in combination with the heat.

To save the collections in the cellar from being drowned, the fire brigade used as little water as possible, a tactic that proved successful. When the cellar was opened, about 40 hours after the fire started, it was clear that the water damage was minimal. But there were problems with the heat radiating from the remains of the fire above. Quite soon, it was obvious that the temperature was increasing and the relative humidity dropping. About six hours from the opening, the temperature had reached nearly 85° centigrade, and the rH (relative humidity) dropped to only 10 percent. To meet this problem, a hole was opened up in one of the cellar walls and fresh air was blown through the cellar.

Before the evacuation of the collections, the roof had to be reinforced to secure it from collapsing. In waiting for the "green light," the evacuation was planned in detail.

The evacuation was executed by a local company that specialized in cleaning up after fires. The cellar collections were packed in corrugated cardboard boxes according to instructions from the library and the archives. It all seemed to work out very well. The transportation boxes were marked with ID numbers and piled on loading pallets to be transported to an acceptable depository located near the city.

Because of the situation, it was only possible to make spot tests to find out if there was damage to the saved collections from the extreme heat and dryness. As you would expect, there was shrinking and cracking damage on some books covered with leather or parchment, as a result of the heat and dryness. The covers were curling heavily or the joints had broken. A little bit surprisingly, the old handwritten parchment letters seemed to be in good shape, even the wax seals! [Perhaps] a result of the way they were stored, in boxes? Old globes, maps, and photos also looked unaffected! But there was a collection of newspapers that felt like paper samples after an accelerated aging test: stiff and inflexible. The stacks of newspapers were still warm, and there was a strong smell of groundwood paper among those shelves.

A small amount of the books in the cellar were damaged from water. To avoid mold growth, they were packed, individually surrounded with plastic, in boxes and sent to a huge freezer, belonging to a local ice-cream company(!), while waiting for treatment.

The rescue operation seemed to us well planned, and the rescue committee had so far made great work. On the first day after the fire, my colleague Per Cullhed was already in contact with the coordinator for the rescue work, to give him "first aid" advice.

To make a conclusion to this message, you could say that the library and the archives were lucky to have rescued the older collections. Despite the extreme situation in the cellar, there was surprisingly little visible damage to the materials. But there will probably be some of that in the future. Or to quote my colleague Ingmar Frojd, when we were feeling the "well-baked" volumes of old newspapers in our hands, "There went another 100 years!"

Aftermath of the Disaster

In a private communication from Lars Bjordal, written two weeks after the original report, he sums up the experience and how the library and archives are "returning to normal."[2]

The rescue work is all finished now and it all went well. But, unfortunately, it looks like there were no books to be saved under the collapsed roof on the main building, as we hoped for. It means that the unique collection on literature from this county of Sweden was lost in the fire. The planning for the restoration of the library has begun; meanwhile, the library staff are "put in school" to learn more on working with computers and the Internet. The intention is to come out of the crisis as the most modern library in Sweden. And it is very important, especially for the staff, to have a new positive goal to work for! The library has had great support from a health care company specializing in helping other companies and official workplaces with all questions concerning health problems—from how to be aware of dangerous chemicals and physical illness to the mental condition of the staff. It usually happens that the companies rent this service, which gives the institution the right to use the expertise from the health care company, drawing on the doctors, nurses, psychologists, physiotherapists, engineers, and chemists. The first days after the fire, the library staff was already put under "therapy" from psychologists, so they could work on the mental problems that always come after a disaster like this. It is very important that all the staff are put on this therapy.

Some recent information on the Linkoping library fire story (as of August 31, 1999) appears below[3]:

> The first step was taken a year ago for the rebuilding of the library. Almost like the bird Phoenix, a new building will rise from the ashes and will be ready to open in January 2000. As I mentioned in my report two years ago, the staff has been through several courses on computers and the Internet, so when the library opens it will turn out as a modern IT-library, ready to meet the demands for the new millennium. In the meantime, the book collection has been reconstructed as completely as possible. As a part of that work, our library has contributed to the conservation and bookbinding work on an older collection that was partly damaged. Over a thousand books have been gone through by hand for cleaning and restoring burned parts of the books. It has taken over a year with one person working full time. This project has been financed by some of the insurance money that we received as a result of the fire (approximately $60,000). To avoid future catastrophes, the Swedish National Library has begun an initiative for a national preservation plan, where disaster planning has a central position. The first step for this national plan will be to take an inventory of all library collections in Sweden. And when the library collection map is drawn, the work on how to preserve them for the future will take place. In the meantime, one hopes that nothing else happens, because the inventory work probably will take some years.

Endnotes

1. "Fire in Linkoping Library," ConsDist.Lst 10:34, October 3, 1996, available online at http://palimpsest. Stanford.edu. (ConsDist.Lst is an electronic discussion list that focuses on issues in conservation and preservation.) The text was edited with permission from Lars Bjordal.

2. Lars Bjordal, "Re: Summary of Fire in Linkoping," e-mail to the author, October 18, 1996. Available e-mail: mbkcons@netexp.net.

3. E-mail from Lars Bjordal, August 31, 1999.

Recovery; or, Resumption of Normal Operations

fter all the adrenaline and the high-level energy evoked by the disaster have disappeared from your system, it is time to get down to the business of resuming operations and services. The standing water has been removed from the building, holes in the roof and the windows are covered over, and the undamaged collection is assembled to determine what is "still there." Damaged materials were sent to be dried and cleaned, or are frozen, awaiting funding for cleaning. Other portions of the collection were destroyed in the disaster. Yet another portion is untouched and either in the building or in an alternative location arranged to provide basic services to patrons, clients, and staff.

For some, this will be a time of great creativity and freedom, a time when "we have always done it this way" can be questioned and innovations introduced. This attitude is a natural extension of having to replace portions of the collection that were damaged or destroyed. Other aspects of this attitude arise from the need to provide services quickly and efficiently, allowing for shortcuts and accessing

alternative sources for information. In the long run, these "Band-Aid" methods may become the *new routines*.

Making Decisions

If the building is intact, determine which areas of the building will be open to the public, if any. It is important *not* to open the building to the public until the response phase is completed. This avoids conflicts between "doing my job" and "helping with the disaster response team's job" of cleanup and recovery. Bring up the most important and basic services first. These usually include circulation, basic reference services, and fiscal services. In the case of information systems, the circulation and online catalogs may be the first to be restored, and possibly the website if it is running on the same system. Cataloging operations should follow later. The order for restoring services and operations should have been determined during the prioritization for recovery phase. The order for restoring the computer systems and operations is also decided during the planning phase. Remember that the Information Systems department is going to have its own plan for restoring operations, data, and services. Note the places where the two plans intersect and keep each other informed. At this point, don't re-arrange the order of resumption of services; save this for the evaluation period.

Set up a method for retrieving books from the sections of the collections that are closed to the public. Arrange a schedule so that staff are rotated into public service functions, while at other times they are assisting in the necessary recovery opera-tions, such as evaluating what is left of the collec-tion or supervising any physical cleanup that still needs to be done. As the damaged areas are re-stored, open them to the public one at a time.

It is important to keep an eye on the environ-mental conditions of the library or archives after water damage has been cleaned up. Frequent and routine checks of the temperature and relative hu-midity must be made. The HVAC system should be examined by facilities maintenance staff or the service contractor to make certain it will keep the environment stable. It may require several exami-nations to determine that the HVAC system is working properly. Filters and intake vents should be checked and cleaned, or replaced, to remove any debris lodged within.

After water damage, the collections in the dried-out and the undamaged parts of the building should be checked regularly for mold. This is particularly important during the first year after the water dam-age, as the building continues to dry, and the trapped moisture escapes into the air.[1] A mold infection can occur even six months after the excess water is removed. Check for paint releasing itself from walls and ceilings and watch for floor or carpet tiles com-ing loose and moist or distorted acoustic ceiling tiles. These are all tell-tale signs that moisture is trapped and trying to get out into the building. If staff or pa-trons complain about unusual odors, don't ignore the reports. This is often a sign that moisture is trapped under paint or carpets and mold is growing there.

Simple, no-cost solutions for releasing trapped moisture are removing ceiling tiles, loose floor and carpet tiles and scraping or removing the loose paint from the walls. When the building structure is com-pletely dry, then the walls can be repainted and car-pets and ceiling tiles replaced.

Evaluating the Plan

After services and operations are back to normal, it is time to evaluate the recovery plan. This is an op-portunity to see if the planning worked, if the best decisions were made for dealing with the worst.

Look at the efficiency of the plan. Were the pri-oritization for recovery decisions the best that could have been made? Were the response decisions useful and easy to understand? What was left out? Add the omitted procedures and decisions to the response plan.

Assess and adjust the prioritization for recovery decisions. Were the disaster response team and staff able to determine which sections of the collections were designated for primary and secondary recov-ery? Did you discover that damaged items that were discarded greatly weakened the collections? Were those items that were kept or recovered out-of-date? If yes, did they fit within the mission of the institu-tion? Did the order of restoring services make a dif-ference? Did you discover that an operation was dependent upon some service listed as a lower prior-ity? If so, rearrange the order of recovery of services.

Examine the effectiveness of the disaster re-sponse team members in the operation. Is it necessary to reassign duties? Did you discover a staff member who is incapable of working under stress? Did you discover strengths previously unknown among the staff and disaster response team, such as a great or-ganizer or someone with lots of contacts within the building trades? Do disaster response team members wish to be relieved of the responsibility, and are there others who wish to participate more actively?

Think about what was missing from the response phase of the operation. Were the instructions too complicated? Were there local library/archives pro-fessionals who assisted who were not included on the contact list? If so, add them.

These are just some of the questions to ask after the disaster is over. As you will see in the case study from the Metropolitan Library in Oklahoma City, staff discovered their first aid kits were inadequate for dealing with anything more than a small cut or minor injury. Keeping in mind that the response plan should be *simple and easy to understand*, consider what you would like to add or omit, and do so.

Revising the Response Plan

Now that the plan, disaster response team members, and all assistance from staff and contractors have been evaluated for efficiency, it is time to revise. Change the plan to reflect whatever deficiencies were noted during the evaluation. Amend the plan to reflect the current situation and layout.

Other than after a disaster or crisis, the disaster response plan needs to be revised and updated every year. At least twice a year, the disaster response team should get together to review the response plan, update the disaster response team contact information, check the floor plans for accuracy, and perform a building survey.

Every year the prioritization for recovery list should be sent to department heads for updating. The list should be revised based upon results of the disaster or, if there has never been one, based upon the same criteria as last time. Prioritization for recovery should be updated to include any major additions to the collections, deaccessioning projects, and changes in the mission statement of the institution.

Once each year hold a training session for the disaster response team and new and old staff. Base the training upon any "new issues" that arose based upon experience with a disaster. Try to add new material to the training, focusing on areas where the knowledge base is lacking.

Hold a yearly meeting with the security and facilities maintenance departments to focus on being better prepared for a disaster the next time. Evaluate conflicts that arose during the disaster and how they were handled. Ask for input on how to make the next response effort more efficient. Discuss areas of conflicting responsibility so they are not ignored or efforts duplicated next time. Provide a building walk-through for the security and facilities maintenance departments and disaster response team members to discuss potential hazards. Familiarize them with new configurations in departments and buildings. This cooperative effort and exchange should facilitate a smooth working relationship and open communications among all the parties.

Following Up

It is essential to communicate with staff, administration, vendors/suppliers, and patrons after the disaster and cleanup operation is over. Write articles and memos about what happened. Describe the results of the disaster and any changes to the disaster response plan. Highlight changes to the collection, services, and routines within the departments that were affected and to the institution as a whole. The articles and memos should come either from a single spokesperson within the institution, as when the disaster first occurred, from the disaster response team as a whole, or from the director.

The disaster response team and the director of the institution should make recommendations to the administration and to facilities maintenance, aiming at prevention of future (re)occurrences of disasters. The recommendations should include suggestions about how to prevent disasters in the future by repairing what went wrong in the first place. Solicit input from the outside consultants and contractors and from security and facilities maintenance departments.

When all is said and done, the library director should publicly recognize the efforts of all staff. This will boost morale and encourage the staff to participate wholeheartedly in the next disaster response operation. The director should also thank the facilities maintenance and security departments, and any others involved, for their assistance and participation in the response and cleanup operations.

Dealing with the Next Disaster— Physical and Psychological Issues

The more often disasters occur at an institution, especially if they are spaced closely together, the less the desire of the staff and even the disaster response team to respond and contribute to the recovery of the collection and services. There will be a noticeable lack of motivation and a visible decrease in assistance from within the institution. The number of staff complaints will increase. These complaints may cite that the staff member is "being pulled away from her or his regular responsibilities" to deal with "someone else's" problem. In some cases, the staff member may have been physically affected by a mold outbreak and particulate matter that triggered allergic and asthmatic reactions or exacerbated these conditions. Health issues should be addressed, and if the staff member is not able to work within a disaster situation the next time, his or her duties should be reassigned within the recovery plan. These few staff members could be assigned support or administrative work in an alternative location for the duration of the cleanup operation.

In addition to morale issues, an increase in environmental problems may arise. The temperature and relative humidity may change more frequently and become more difficult to keep stable. Two environmental side effects that may arise are mold and the increased aging of collections. There is a definite chance mold will occur, and it will become more difficult to control its growth and spread, especially if there was water damage. The second side effect results from fluctuations in temperature and relative humidity. As these factors change from day to day, or hour to hour, the collections are in danger of becoming brittle and fragile more quickly than before.[2]

With every fluctuation of temperature and relative humidity, the chemical reactions within paper and photographs start and stop, contributing adversely to the deterioration of the collections.

For the "next" disaster, the disaster response team and the director of the institution might consider more seriously working with outside contractors and consultants. If there were unreasonable physical demands made upon staff, consider contracting out the majority of the physical work, perhaps even the work the facilities maintenance department performs.

With the increased frequency of disasters, there needs to be a concerted effort to correct and control potential hazards and chronic problems that cause disasters. Institute a regular maintenance program to prevent future disasters. After the third or fourth disaster, even a small disaster can be demoralizing.

Disasters where the causes were not eliminated through diligent maintenance and repair are demoralizing and dreaded. In fact, the frequency of occurrence, especially from the same cause, may color and skew thinking and decision making for future renovation and construction projects. For instance, if there is a history of water damage in the building, the tendency is to shy away from any product, such as sprinklers or heating systems, that contains water, even if it would be more efficient. It is important to try to distance oneself from the past when making decisions about construction projects.

CASE STUDY TWO

A Whiff of Mold? No, It Can't Be!

Head Librarian:	"Over the past few months, patrons and staff have been complaining about the smells in section A of the library, some even complaining about headaches and colds."
Head of Facilities Maintenance:	"I don't smell anything out of the ordinary."
Librarian:	"I don't either, but it's getting worse. Even my most dedicated staff member is starting to complain. Can't you do anything about it?"
Head of Facilities Maintenance:	"I'll go look again, but I won't find anything," and off he goes.

Several weeks go by. One day a patron complains to the reference librarian that a book is stuck to the shelf. Could the librarian help him? When the librarian gets to the shelf, the books are indeed stuck, in fact there is lots of mold growing and it really smells. Now the head librarian has something to show the head of facilities maintenance.

At the same time, staff has been complaining about the staff lounge in the basement. It is starting to smell down there, and clothes in the lockers are damp.

So the head librarian and the head of facilities maintenance go on a building inspection to see what is going on. Here's what they found.

The books on the shelf in section A are heavily contaminated with mold, the grey and yellow fuzzy kind. The mold has attached itself to the shelves. The books are damp inside and starting to swell from the excess moisture. That was where there had been a roof leak six months earlier. Everyone thought that the area was dry and the relative humidity was under control. Were they wrong!

In the basement, they discover that the mechanical room is in disarray. The HVAC, chiller, and drain pans are full of water, and the floor drain is clogged, with water in small puddles on the floor. To make matters worse, someone has been storing boxes of cleaning supplies (paper towels and the like) in the mechanical room and everything is damp with a black mold growing on the walls and equipment. Oh boy, what a mess!

What to tackle first? The head librarian activates the disaster response team to deal with the moldy books. The disaster response team contacts a disaster response company to take the books away for drying and cleaning. The disaster response company reminds the disaster response team that the books may come back a little distorted due to the swelling of the bindings. The books have to dry first, and then they will attempt to remove the visible mold. The disaster response team is cautioned that the books may be stained, but as long as the temperature and relative humidity stay dry and stable, the mold should not return. The staff was then directed to clean the shelves with a disinfectant and dry them well.

The mechanical room is a bigger headache. The first action was to remove all the boxes that were stored there. Not only is it a fire hazard, but the boxes were also retaining moisture, which mold just loves. The increased moisture is an invitation for insects such as cockroaches and silver fish. Next, the facilities maintenance department drained and cleaned the chiller and drain pans and the floor drain. An HVAC specialist was called in to look at the equipment and fix it. While the HVAC specialist was recalibrating the system, the head of facilities maintenance sent the person responsible for the library's maintenance to a workshop to learn how to maintain the equipment more efficiently.

Then the mold was dealt with. The head of facilities maintenance and the disaster response team got together to discuss this action. Because staff were complaining about feeling ill, they decided to have an industrial hygienist examine and test the mold in the mechanical room and in the library, especially in section A. The head of the library decided that it was time to call the insurance company and see what they could contribute. The insurance adjuster explained that it was possible that mold wasn't covered. (Some insurance companies are no longer covering remediation of mold, no matter what the cause.) After careful consideration, the insurance adjuster agreed that some of the damage was covered by the policy.

The industrial hygienist sampled the air, the black mold, and the duct work to see what was growing there. The mold was the dreaded *Stachybotrys chartarum (atra)*, the black mold that is highly toxic. The industrial hygienist designed a remediation plan, and a company was hired to clean and remove the active mold from the mechanical room and any duct work that was affected. The HVAC system was shut down, the ducts covered, and the mechanical room was cleaned. Then the ducts were cleaned and the HVAC filters were changed. Lastly, the HVAC was recalibrated to maintain the proper stable temperature and relative humidity.

While all this was going on, the staff asked the librarian for some education and training. They wanted to understand about the mold, the health implications, and whether the building was safe to work in. The librarian and the disaster response team head decided to bring in some consultants to talk about mold and the remediation of mold. The consultants focused on what causes mold growth and how it is controlled inside. They discussed the importance of steady temperatures and relative humidity as well as adequate air movement. The health issues discussed included discomfort from the mold and exacerbation of allergies and asthma. Any staff member who had complained was sent for a checkup. As the building and air-handling system were cleaned, there were fewer complaints.

Once the mechanical room and section A were decontaminated, the industrial hygienist was again called in to sample the air, walls, and ducts to see what the mold content was. All was back to normal after six long months of work. The now dry and clean books were brought back in and shelved. The mechanical room was outfitted with water sensors on the floor and next to the chiller and drain pans.

So What Do We Learn from This Story?

The first lesson is to follow up on complaints of moldy smells and physical discomfort. If left unchecked, mold can infect a building completely, requiring it be closed during remediation. Ignoring health complaints can exacerbate asthma and allergies, resulting in long illnesses and even requiring a leave of absence from the library.

The second lesson is to perform an internal building survey regularly. Check the mechanical room, the storage closets, and other lesser used rooms to make certain the environment is stable and there aren't any water leaks. Invite the maintenance staff along on these building surveys so that all are looking for the same problems and issues of maintenance and environmental control.

The third is to act on the problems. Hire the specialists to do specialized jobs. Don't expect your staff to remove large areas of mold growth. They are not prepared or trained to do so.

In the midst of it all, don't forget to communicate with staff. Let them know what is happening and how the problem is being fixed. Active, two-way communication goes a long way toward solving issues before they become a problem or a major source of complaint.

This case study is a compilation of several mold outbreaks in different institutions, not at any particular library.

Endnotes

1. It is common to have moisture trapped in plaster or concrete walls.

2. James M. Reilly, Douglas W. Nishimura, and Edward Zinn, *New Tools for Preservation: Assessing Long-Term Environmental Effects on Library and Archives Collections* (Washington, D.C.: Commission on Preservation and Access, 1995). See, especially, p. 10–14.

Prevention

s stated in the introduction, prevention can stand alone, but it also works in tandem with the planning phase of disaster response. Prevention includes looking for potential hazards in the building and either noting or correcting them. This phase is important because correcting chronic problems before they become serious can prevent them from becoming a disaster and costing the institution large sums of money and loss of time and efficient service. In the case of a small library, archives, historical society, or corporate library, prevention and planning for disasters can mean the difference between existing and being defunct.

So where do you start? Because prevention and planning go together, a disaster response team should be selected ahead of time (see section 4, "Planning"); otherwise, select a small group of key personnel to perform these tasks.

Two types of surveys should take place during the prevention phase of disaster response planning: a building survey and a survey to identify vulnerable collections. For now let us focus upon a building survey.

The Building Survey

Depending upon the size of the institution and the number of buildings covered by the plan, a building survey can be done by one member of the disaster response team or by groups of staff headed by a team member. In either case, the purpose and procedures are the same.

The purpose of a building survey is to look for evidence of past disasters (for example, old water damage, which should be easy to find) and areas of the library or archives that are potential disasters.

Plan to draw a basic floor plan that locates fire exits and identifies rooms as to their purpose or contents during the survey. Ultimately, the floor plan will show where the first and second priority collections are located for removal or recovery. Remember that the library staff may not be able to enter the building and might have to show firefighters or a disaster response company where the most vulnerable and valuable items are that require removal and treatment.

Start the survey by looking at emergency exits to determine if they are accessible.

- Emergency exits should be visible and clearly marked.

- Make certain the exit signs and doors are not blocked and that the alarms on the doors, if any, work.

- It is important to ask where the alarms ring—in the immediate vicinity or throughout the building.

- Does the alarm ring or light up in a central security office, and if so, do the security people know whom to call in an emergency?

Other security and safety items to check are emergency lighting (do the batteries still work and how often are they replaced?); fire extinguishers (both location and type); fire alarm call boxes (where are they located?); and smoke and heat alarms (do they meet the appropriate needs of the collections in those areas, and where do the alarms ring?).

The next step is to look for past and potential hazards such as water leaks; old and chronic leaks are sometimes identified by brown staining on ceiling tiles or leaching of minerals on walls. Water stains indicate that there was a problem and could occur again or that something is dripping on a regular basis, such as an air-conditioning duct that gets too much condensation and doesn't drain properly. A stain might indicate a small leak in the roof or flashing that allows water to get into the building when it rains. Routine inspections of the roof should be done by the facilities maintenance staff. Side effects of chronic water leaks include structural damage and weakening of walls and ceilings. Under the right conditions, fluctuations in the environment, in combination with a chronic leak, could create mold growth. When undetected, mold can spread through a sizable portion of the collection, infecting the air-handling system as well as causing staff discomfort.

Indicate chronic problem areas on the floor plan. Discuss the identification of the source of the water leak(s), and work with the facilities maintenance staff to correct the situation.

Another potential hazard includes use and storage of flammable chemicals in the library or build-ing. Emphasize that the chemicals must be stored in fireproof cabinets when not in use and that appropriate handling and precautions be incorporated when used. Keep a file of Material Safety Data Sheets (MSDS) for easy reference should an accident occur (see figure 3.1 for page 1 of the six-page form). Material Safety Data Sheets include handling and cleanup information as well as a list of ingredients. Supplies and collections should not be stored in stairwells and hallways. They are a fire hazard and may prevent firefighters and disaster response personnel from entering the building quickly and efficiently.

Walk through the building(s) with the regular facilities maintenance staff and ask them to point out where they see potential hazards or where they routinely fix problems. Ask them to show you where the sprinkler water control valve is located, and make certain that it is properly activated and maintained. Ask where the shutoff valves are located for the gas, electricity, and water. These should be listed in the checklist for the building. Discuss the reasons for disaster response planning with facilities maintenance staff. Ask where and how they see themselves participating in the response and recovery aspects of the plan.

Do the same with the security staff, looking for potential security problems, including identifying doors and windows that don't shut properly. Discuss the reasons for disaster response planning with the security staff. Ask where and how they see themselves participating in the response and recovery aspects of the plan.

Next, the disaster response team and someone from facilities maintenance should walk around the outside of the building, looking for potential water and fire hazards. Notice where there are external stairs going below ground. The drains at the bottom of those stairs should be cleaned regularly to prevent water backing up into the foundation or the basement level. Locate the external fresh air intake shafts. They are large grates set into the ground or walls. They should be clear of debris such as leaves and bushes. Keeping the fresh air intakes clear will decrease indoor air quality problems. Talk with facilities maintenance staff about their regular exter-

FIGURE 3.1. Page 1 of Material Safety Data Sheet. The form covers fire and explosion data, health effects data, spill and leak procedures, etc.

Material Safety Data Sheet May be used to comply with OSHA's Hazard Communication Standard, 29 CFR 1910.1200. Standard must be consulted for specific requirements.	U.S. Department of Labor Occupational Safety and Health Administration (Non-Mandatory Form) Form Approved OMB No. 1218-0072	◈

IDENTITY (As Used on Label and List) GF‡ GB6N	Note: Blank spaces are not permitted. If any item is not applicable, or no information is available, the space must be marked to indicate that.

Section I

Manufacturer's Name GLUE-FAST EQUIPMENT CO., INC	Emergency Telephone Number (201) 939-7100
Address (Number, Street, City, State, and ZIP Code) 727 COMMERCIAL AVE	Telephone Number for Information SAME
CARLSTADT, NJ 07072	Date Prepared JUNE 1989
	Signature of Preparer (optional)

Section II — Hazardous Ingredients/Identity Information

Hazardous Components (Specific Chemical Identity; Common Name(s))	OSHA PEL	ACGIH TLV	Other Limits Recommended	% (optiona

NONE HAZARDOUS

---

3. PHYSICAL DATA

```
PURE MATERIAL OR MIXTURE.........  Mixture
PHYSICAL FORM....................  Liquid
APPEARANCE/PHYSICAL DESCRIPTION..  White liquid, typical slight sweet odor
PH AS IS.........................  7.5  per JSullivan/Gluefast 3/31/92
BOILING-POINT....................  >212 F
MELTING/FREEZING POINT...........  <40 F
SOLUBILITY IN WATER..............  Miscible
SPECIFIC GRAVITY (WATER = 1).....  1.100
BULK DENSITY.....................  9.2 lb/gal
VOLATILES........................  49%/wt
EVAPORATION RATE.................  1 ( Water )
VAPOR PRESSURE (mmHg)............  17.5 at 20 c
VAPOR DENSITY (AIR = 1)..........  0.62
VOLATILE ORGANIC COMPOUNDS.......  <5g/l
```

nal cleaning routines. Gutters and eaves should be cleaned regularly to prevent water backup under the roof or into foundations. Pay particular attention to any mention of damage to the roof. Look for broken or cracked windows. Note windows that aren't shut completely. The same goes for external doors. Pay particular attention to emergency exit doors. They should never be propped open or obstructed. Follow up on any damage or potential problems that are scheduled to be fixed.

Correcting and Preventing Fire and Safety Hazards

After the potential hazards have been identified, it is important to consider how to remedy the situations and prevent disasters from ever coming to fruition. Store flammable chemicals properly, house collections in appropriate areas of the building, and perform regular maintenance to prevent damage from external sources. Set up a routine for regularly walking through the building(s) and checking on these safety and maintenance points.

After looking at the building, review the fire prevention equipment, its type and its location. This includes fire extinguishers, sprinklers, and smoke and heat detectors.

Fire Extinguishers

The two types of fire extinguishers found in libraries and archives are ABC and A. The canister has a label on it that tells you the type of fire extinguisher. There should also be a tag attached to the metal ring at the top of the handle. This tag indicates when the fire extinguisher was checked last.

If you must use a fire extinguisher to put out a very small fire, make certain it is the proper type. Class A fires consist of ordinary combustible materials such as wood, paper, rubber, cloth, and some plastics. Class B fires come from flammable liquids, paints, flammable gases, and other types of liquids. Class C fires occur around energized electrical equipment, such as computers and office equipment; B and C canisters contain foam. The larger fire extinguisher canisters are usually type A, and they may contain water. Fire extinguishers have enough contents under pressure to work for 30 seconds to a few minutes. If there is too much fire, leave the building and call the fire department.

Sprinkler Systems and Smoke and Heat Detectors

Why is it important to have sprinklers in the library? Fire sprinklers, especially if they are zoned (that is, only those sprinklers in the immediate area of the fire activate), will cause less damage to the collection than fire hoses. Each fire sprinkler head puts out between 20 to 40 gallons of water per minute; a fire hose, wielded by firefighters, will put out more than 250 gallons of water per minute. Also, without fire sprinklers, the collection could be consumed by fire before the fire department can get to the building, even if the fire station is across the street or next door.

There are two main types of fire sprinkler systems: wet pipe and dry pipe. Wet pipe systems have water in them all the time, waiting for a fire to erupt so that they can release their load. Dry pipe systems come in a variety of types. Either there is compressed air in the pipes or nothing. When the sprinkler head is opened or activated by either the fire or the smoke detector, after about a two-minute delay, water flows into the pipe and then comes out of the head. Consider on/off sprinkler heads for both wet and dry pipe sprinkler systems in museums and archives. These heads are more expensive than the standard type. They turn on to emit water and put out the fire and then turn off. If the fire flares up again, the sprinkler head will reopen.

With the banning of new installations of Halon 1301, there has been an increase in the popularity of a new sprinkler system called "Water Mist" or Micromist, which emits fine water droplets under high pressure of 100 to 1,000 psi or approximately two gallons of water per minute. Already in use on ships and in the oil drilling industry, this method of fire suppression is being considered for museums and other cultural institutions, where Halon was the norm.[1]

There are different types of smoke detectors. Some detect changes in temperature, others detect increased particulate matter in the air. It is imperative that there be smoke detectors and alarms in libraries and archives. But more important than being installed and working properly, is that the alarm rings somewhere other than just inside the building. Who will hear it in the middle of the night if the smoke alarm just rings inside the building or in the basement? The smoke detectors and alarms should be tied into the general alarm system and should be able to trigger the fire sprinkler system to put out the fire.

Regardless of which system is installed in the library or archives, several features should be present:

- The smoke and heat alarms need to be tied to the activation of the sprinkler system.
- Smoke detectors and alarms must ring outside the building as well as inside.
- The sprinklers must be zoned, so that only the one or two sprinkler heads over the fire are activated.
- Sprinkler heads should shut off automatically when the fire is out and reactivate themselves if the fire flares up again.

Members of the disaster response team should know where the fire sprinkler shutoff valves are and should indicate their location on the basic floor plan.

If there are no sprinklers in the building because of its age, smoke detectors and alarms are even more important. Establish a routine to check regularly that they are in good working order and that the staff know who to call, and where to meet outside the building, when the fire alarms sound.

Indoor Air Quality and Sick Building Syndrome

So far we have looked for visible potential hazards in the building. An invisible hazard is poor indoor air quality that can manifest itself in *sick building syndrome*.

Every time something is done in or to the library or the building that houses it, there is the potential to create an imbalance in the internal environment. These changes can cause the collection to deteriorate more quickly, can exacerbate allergies and make the staff sick, or can cause water damage to the building through carelessness or accident. Buildings that have windows that don't open, have chronic maintenance problems, or have experienced a water-related disaster are prime candidates for sick building syndrome.

The most common type of sick building syndrome and indoor air quality problem for cultural institutions is *mold*. It is present, all the time, in the air and on most surfaces, but mold does not cause a concern or problem until it becomes active. Poor environmental conditions, increased levels of moisture, and high humidity act together and separately to encourage mold growth. Mold likes warm, moist, dark places and will grow in carpets, under paint, in air ducts, and on collections. When mold growth is not controlled, it can cause a sick building.

Two basic procedures can prevent and remove mold growth, but it is important to realize that mold is never truly eradicated.

1. Keep the temperature and relative humidity stable:
   - Temperatures should be between 68° and 72° Fahrenheit and the relative humidity between 45 percent and 55 percent, but no higher than 65 percent.
   - In the winter it is sometimes difficult to keep the relative humidity above 35 percent. Discuss the dryness of the air with your conservation or preservation staff to determine the degree of damage this causes.
2. Act quickly if there is a leak or water damage:
   - Fix the leak or cause of water damage.
   - Remove the water as quickly as possible.
   - Use dehumidifiers to control excess moisture and to help stabilize the environment.

Once the standing water is removed, it is essential to stabilize the environment. It may be necessary to hire a dehumidification firm to provide temporary assistance or rental of equipment. While the building is drying, monitor the temperature stability and relative humidity with a recording hygrograph. If the relative humidity goes above 65 percent, watch for additional outbreaks of mold.

Additional steps should be taken to prevent the spread of mold throughout the building. If the mold is localized in one room or area, cover the air vents and ducts to prevent mold from spreading into the entire building. The next step in the recovery operation is to arrest mold growth by stabilizing the environment or freezing the infected portion of the collection.

Remove the mold to prevent serious problems for both the collections and the staff. After covering the air vents, begin the mold-removal process. Clean the infected collection, shelves, walls, carpets, and other affected furnishings. Be careful not to introduce moisture, or increase the relative humidity, or mold *will* grow again. These collections will be sensitive to mold forever and can become infected again if the relative humidity rises above 65 percent to 70 percent.

If the cause of the water damage is not eliminated, then mold will return again and again. Each time, it will be more pervasive, more difficult to remove, and more damaging to the collection. Constant disaster response for mold removal will create morale problems for staff who must repeat the process. Unfortunately, mold irritates allergies and exacerbates asthma. It can cause healthy staff to develop, first, a sensitivity to mold and, then, allergies.

Reactions to mold may vary from a stuffy nose and flu-like symptoms to coughing, sneezing, and discomfort—the most common symptoms of an allergic reaction. It is important to keep track of these health complaints as they are signs of a potential sick building or a possible mold infection in the air-handling system. If there are a number of complaints, the air ducts and the HVAC system should be checked for mold. Clean and disinfect the air-handling system appropriately. The Environmental Protection Agency and Occupational Safety and Health Administration have guidelines and regulations for monitoring and treating indoor air quality problems.

After the mold is removed and the environment is under control, replace the filters in the air-handling system. It is essential to use the correct filters and to replace them on a regular basis.

Mold is not the only cause of sick building syndrome, nor the only factor that can affect indoor air quality. Paint fumes, cleaning fluids, air pollution, fumes from adhesives in carpets and furniture, and ozone from equipment also contribute to create poor indoor air quality, but these issues are beyond the scope of this book.

Remote Storage Facilities

When performing the building survey, it is important to check the collections stored outside the main building.

As available storage in the primary building decreases, there is a corresponding increase in the need for remote storage facilities. There are two main types of remote storage: the first is a facility built especially for this purpose and owned by the institution itself or by a consortium of institutions in the same geographical area. The second is a rented building or designated space that may not have been built for this specific purpose. Some rented spaces were designed to be record storage facilities; others are just warehouses. The former is better for storage of library, archives, and museum collections as there should be built-in environmental controls and fire safety precautions.

What types of disasters are remote storage facilities vulnerable to? Fluctuations in environment, temperature, and relative humidity, if not monitored properly, will decrease the potential life span of all the materials. The contents are under risk of mold or increased physical deterioration due to pollution or particulate matter (which can cause scratches on surfaces, discoloration, or increased aging). Physical damage from improperly installed stacks and shelving is also a possibility. Bookcases properly secured to walls and floors are crucial if the stacks are high, mobile, or in earthquake zones. Stacks should be braced across the top shelves to prevent a domino effect if the ground shifts.

In remote storage facilities, the stacks are often two or three stories tall. These stacks consist of high, industrial shelving designed to hold little-used book collections or archival collections and are accessed from mechanized lifts. The shelf materials should be of appropriate strength, and the structure should be balanced for the appropriate height and weight. Flooding is always a possibility if the remote storage facility is in a flood zone and drainage and excess water pumping ability were not planned for. Check for sump pumps, especially in remote storage facilities that are built below ground or below grade.

Note the following common characteristics of remote and off-site storage facilities:

- They are physically separate from the main collection, usually in a different building.
- If built for remote storage, the structure should not have regular water pipes running across the collections. Wet pipe sprinkler systems should not be a problem. Trouble comes more often

from a faulty sprinkler head than from leaks in the pipes. *The sprinkler system must be zoned.*

- If the facility was built for remote storage, the utilities are usually concentrated in one area; therefore, water and fire hazards are minimal. Only HVAC ducts will run across the building. Watch for condensation in the summer.
- The environment should be stable and controllable, due to limited visitors, less random exchange of air, etc.
- If the remote or off-site storage involves a rented space or a contracted service, then there is minimal control over environment or physical condition of the collection. Special environmental conditions should be discussed at the time of contracting the space, and regular visits should confirm that the environment and physical conditions are as requested.

Survey the remote storage facilities for the following:

- Physical layout
- Collection locations
- Utilities
- Potential hazards (should be minimal)

Establish prioritization during the planning phase:

- Examine the types of collections stored there:
  Low use collections
  Archives and paper records
  Data and magnetic media
  All of the above
- Rank the value to the whole collection (where does this collection fit into the scheme of things, and what level is it prioritized at?).
- Indicate if the collections stored there are from the institution or if it is a shared or regional facility.

The remote storage facility should be treated the same as the main building(s) during the planning phase:

- Survey the building for potential hazards.
- Prioritize the collection for recovery.

- Create floor plans identifying and locating the utilities; collections, with their associated priorities for recovery; and emergency exits.
- Identify personnel who are familiar with the remote storage facility collections and the building layout. These persons (usually the head of the remote storage facility and the second in command) should be able to gain access to the building after hours.
- Create a basic disaster response plan using the remote storage facility personnel as key disaster response team members.
- If the remote storage facility is a rented or contracted service, then the emergency contact personnel names and 24-hour emergency numbers should be included in the disaster response plan, along with the names and numbers of the institution's liaisons.
- Include a map and directions of how to locate the remote storage facility, together with identification of main and auxiliary entrances, in the disaster response plan.
- Establish a schedule for inspection of the facility and the collections. This inspection should be more frequent than for the main collections, as "out of sight, out of mind" definitely holds true in this case.

Backup Routines to Prevent Loss of Computer Data

The more computer- and data-dependent the institution, the more important it is to make copies of data and software on a regular basis. A number of methods can be used. The backup method depends upon the size of the insitution, library, or archives; the amount of computer activity; and the types of services provided.

If the only data on the computer are letters and payroll records, then back up the data on diskettes (other than the one that holds the data) whenever the data are altered, and store the diskettes off-site or in another location in the building.

If the library, archives, or information center uses data heavily and has large databases, then a regular backup routine is required. A tape backup is the most effective and economical. Back up new data at the end of each day. If the data are critical or sensitive, back up the data more often. This incremental backup routine is important for inventory or cataloging operations or database tagging and input. Keep in mind that it takes a day to reconstruct each hour of lost data.

If the library is hooked into a mainframe or local area network (LAN), determine how often the system is backed up and confirm that the library is included on a regular basis.

The most common method of routine backup for large scale operations is the "Grandfather" rotation. It consists of daily incremental backup routines, that is, copying the data or files accessed or changed that day. Using your backup software program, copy that data onto the tape every day. On Friday, copy the entire file set, keep that tape, and store it off-site. This routine is repeated on the used tape every day for a month, keeping the Friday and full backup tapes separate. Perform a full backup on the last day of the month and store it as a "month end." The tapes can be kept as monthly or quarterly compilations, depending upon space and data constraints.

Ideally, only the day's data will be lost if the disaster occurs during working hours. No data are lost if the disaster occurs at night after the backup is performed. Backup tapes should be stored in a fireproof location, either at an off-site data center or data vault. Fireproof cabinets do not necessarily protect tapes, as they can melt at 125° Fahrenheit. The full backup tapes should be checked to make certain that the data can be read and imported should the need arise. Faulty tapes are just as bad as no backup at all.

Don't forget to make a copy of the operating and program software, both commercial and custom, and store it off-site with the data. These copies will be important if the entire system is lost or inaccessible.

Establish a testing routine to practice uploading or importing data to the software. Test the routine at least once a year, if not more often. Write out these routines in simple language in case the expert in the department is not available on the day of the disaster.

Remember that business interruption insurance and extra expense insurance riders usually do not include funds for reconstructing lost data. The insurance company assumes that data are backed up on a regular basis and are accessible, readable, and importable, should it become necessary. The insurance company also assumes that an institution with extensive computer needs has contracted with a hot or cold site—a location designed for operating a computer system off-site on a temporary basis. A business interruption insurance rider should cover the costs of computer rental. Check the policy to confirm that it covers your computing needs.

Survey to Identify Vulnerable Collections

After surveying the building(s), you will have identified where there is a potential for damage. At this point it is important to identify collections that are vulnerable to water or heat. Materials that fit this description include early photographic processes, especially nitrate film; phonograph records and other forms of early audio recordings; all magnetic tapes, whether audio, video, or computer; and, most prevalent, clay-coated paper. These collections are in the most danger of total destruction when there is a disaster involving fire or water.

Early photographic processes are very water sensitive. If the photographs sit in water, it is possible for the adhesive that binds the image to the base to release and allow the image to slide off. Wet collodion negatives are very sensitive to water and are difficult to recover. This process includes ambrotypes and tintypes. Daguerreotypes are also sensitive to water. If the institution has nitrate film, it should *not only* be stored separately from all other collections, *but also* should be protected from water. When decomposing, nitrate film is flammable. Contact the fire department before disposing of nitrate film. Let the fire department know if the area where nitrate film is stored is involved in the disaster. Mark the boxes with early photographic processes to indicate two things: *water sensitive* and *heavy*. Nitrate film should be labeled clearly. Make certain the boxes are stored in areas that have the least potential for water damage.

Early phonograph cylinders are made of water-sensitive materials. Some of the materials are wax, acrylic plastics, and acetate. Pre-1950 phonograph records have a base of anything from cardboard and acetate to glass and metal. Some of the materials are sensitive to water, others to heat. Most phonograph records will withstand *some* water, but they should be removed from it and dried as quickly as possible. Acrylic phonograph records are sensitive to heat and may melt. Mark containers of metal and glass phonograph records to indicate that they are heavy.

Magnetic tape is sensitive to extremes of heat. At about 125° Fahrenheit, most forms of magnetic tape will start to melt. It is important to realize that computer backup tapes will be damaged irreparably if stored in a room that has no fire-protection system. Fireproof cabinets and safes may be sufficient to keep tapes from melting if the temperature does not rise above the rating for the safe; however, they are not airtight and may permit the entrance of dust and soot. Magnetic tapes can be dried and cleaned if imbedded with soot, dirt, or dust. However, it is not possible to ensure that data are not damaged if the surface is abraded or scratched.

After you have identified the collections that are water and heat sensitive, indicate where they are on the floor plan. This way the disaster response team will know where the most vulnerable collections are and which need to be removed first.

Construction and Renovation Projects

Construction and renovation projects should raise a flag indicating a disaster response plan needs to be created or the current one revised. This is the time when your institution's collections and structure are most vulnerable to damage. Plan for several types of disasters: fire from electrical and mechanical equipment; water damage from open roofs and walls; and mold and mildew. There will be increased levels of dust, dirt, and pollution created by the act of construction itself. Lack of control of the environment (temperature and relative humidity) means an increased risk of mold infections that may not be able to be controlled until the building is sealed again. And let us not forget power and telecommunications outages.

When planning a renovation or construction project, consider the vulnerability of the collection, what parts of the collection are closest to the construction, and how they might be adversely affected. If you choose to move a vulnerable part of the collection, determine the following:

- Where will you store it?
- How will you access it?
- When will it be returned to its original or new location?
- How many areas of the collection will be moved, and how many times?
- Can the collection withstand the move and the change in environmental conditions?
- What about the costs, inconvenience, staffing issues, and the environment of the temporary location?

If you decide to leave the collection in place during construction or renovation in the building, take precautions to protect the collection:

- Cover the collection with plastic sheeting to protect from dust and debris and maintain air flow to prevent mold growth.
- Some libraries and archives shrink-wrap their collections if they are in remote storage facilities or if the area is under construction. The shrink-wrap film is very thin and is gas impermeable. It also protects against water and dust particles.[2]
- Make certain that the dust and debris generated by the construction do not enter the air-handling system. Check and see where the intake air goes—into the ceiling or into ductwork. If the latter is the case, then the ducts should be closed off in the areas where the construction is occurring. If the air goes into the ceiling (also known as an *open plenum system*), then the space between the "false" ceiling and the "true" ceiling needs to be closed off to prevent moving the debris through the building.
- Separate the construction area from the rest of the building. If possible, use a fireproof material to separate the two areas.

- Confirm that the building will stay warm enough during construction so that the pipes do not freeze and crack, causing water damage.

- Seal openings in walls and roofs at the end of each day to prevent water damage from rain or snow. Tarps must be anchored securely and have drainage so that they don't fill with water and then collapse into the building, causing water damage.

Next look at the possible hazards from changes in the environment. When there is construction or renovation in a building, the building envelope is often broken. The *building envelope* allows for control of the temperature, relative humidity, and pollution. There will be an increased amount of dust, dirt, and debris in the building and entering the air-handling, or HVAC, system. Is the system designed to handle the increase? Can it or will it be modified for the duration of the construction? No matter what, the filters will need to be changed more often; change them once again when the building is resealed and the construction cleanup is completed.

Discuss with the facilities maintenance staff and the construction supervisor how they will control or minimize fluctuations in temperature and relative humidity. Will the building be open or relatively open to the outside for a long period of time? If so, temperature- and mold-sensitive collections need to be moved to a different part of the building or a different location. When the construction and the cleanup are completed, the HVAC system will require restabilizing to ensure minimal fluctuations in temperature and relative humidity.

During a renovation or construction project, security should be increased, especially if the construction is going on when the building is closed or regular staff are not present. Security staff should be alert for theft of collections and equipment and should know who has access to the main building and its collections, especially after hours. The security staff should watch for water, fire, or other types of damage and should have contact information for the disaster response team leader.

Steps to be taken during construction should include the following:

- All steps necessary to control the potential damage

- An increased number and regularity of inspections of the collections to make certain they are not being adversely affected by the changes in environment and physical conditions

- An increased awareness on the part of the staff, the disaster response team, the facilities maintenance staff, and the construction workers that fire and water damage are risks that must be avoided

- An edict that smoking, eating, and drinking should be restricted to one area, if not outside the building

- Regular removal of debris, garbage, and food

Take the time to discuss vulnerability of the collections and the building with the head of the construction crew or the senior supervisor. Ask what types of precautions they take to prevent fire and water damage. Provide them with disaster response team emergency contact information in the event of a disaster. Assign a disaster response team or staff member to be the liaison between the construction crews and the library, thereby allowing open communications.

Outside Contacts

Whether there is a preservation librarian on staff or not, that person is not always an expert in conservation nor proficient in dealing with the recovery of all formats in the collection. There are plenty of experts in the field of conservation who deal with special or non-print formats such as photographs, paintings, and furniture. Keep in mind when you read professional literature or attend seminars that the authors and speakers may be experts in their fields. Put their names and contact information on a list. When the disaster occurs—or better yet, beforehand—contact them and ask if they perform conservation work. If they don't, ask for a referral.

If there is a special or rare collection at your institution, find out the names of several conservators who could help you recover the collection from water or fire damage.

Identify conservation centers in the area or the country that specialize in the formats that are most difficult to deal with. Ask them what their "disaster response" policy is and how they can help your institution. Ask for references and check them out for reliability and performance. Determine what services the consultants and conservators can provide, how to contact them, and what their fees are. Confirm that you can add them to the emergency contact list.

If your institution has an unusual collection, consider asking the consultant or conservator to visit and see what is there. Discuss the potential damage that water or fire carry and what recovery treatments might cost. Ask for preventative measures to ensure a minimum amount of damage from fire and water. Learn how to provide basic treatment or stabilization of the items should they be damaged by water. The conservator might suggest storage in a different area or off-site when not in use.

Create a list of consultants and conservators who can deal with different damaged formats in your collection. Place this list in the back of your disaster response plan and consult it when a disaster occurs.

Other professional contacts to add to your disaster response plan are consultants who specialize in assisting institutions in recovering from disasters, writing disaster response plans, and training in recovery of water- and fire-damaged items. Always have extra names on the list so that if the primary contact is unavailable, there is another to call.

Prevention is the best way to head off a disaster. The next case study describes a disaster that occurred during a construction and renovation project.[3] Disasters are not always caused by fire and water. Carelessness, lack of forethought, and lack of control, especially during construction projects, can wreak havoc on carefully stabilized environmental conditions in both general and special collections.

CASE STUDY THREE

Renovation Disaster

In a major cultural institution, a small renovation project was under way in the basement of its four-story library. A quarter of the floor was being converted from office and storage space to a multimedia learning center. To this end, after the room was gutted, the electrical contractors came in to dig trenches in the concrete to lay electrical conduit for computers. All the work took place over a long weekend while the library was closed. When the staff returned on Tuesday, there was concrete dust throughout the entire building, including in the special collections and archives areas. What happened? How can you remove the concrete dust from the collections and the air-handling system?

Let's start with a proactive and preventive approach. First of all, the contractors should have sealed off the rooms where they were sawing concrete from the rest of the library. "Of course they did this!" you say. "Well, 'kind of,'" I must answer. There was a plastic wall erected between the renovated area and the rest of the library; however, *no one* checked to see what was going on in the ceiling. Most ceilings are dropped ceilings—that is, the walls go up much higher and the acoustic tiles hide the air-handling system, electrical wires and plumbing, sprinkler pipes, etc. This area, between the dropped ceiling and true ceiling, was not separated from the rest of the building. That is the first thing the construction crew should have done. The second thing the contractors should have done was turn off the air-handling system while they worked, which they didn't do. So, the concrete dust was picked up by the air intakes and spread throughout the building. A fine layer of dust on every surface, horizontal and vertical, greeted the staff on Tuesday morning. Of course, it was the worst in the basement, where the special collections were kept; but, nonetheless, there was dust on every piece of equipment, computer, and book in the entire building.

Now what? What would you do if called in to deal with the situation?

The first thing to do is make certain *no water* is used to clean up the concrete. Water would make the concrete solidify, perhaps making it impossible to remove.

Gross cleaning efforts were under way almost immediately so that the collections and equipment could be used. Wet/dry vacuums with hepa-filters (very fine filters that capture extremely small dust particles) were utilized to clean the horizontal surfaces and to remove surface dust from the collections. This worked quickly and efficiently on the upper floors. Because the entire library is scheduled for renovation in the next few years and all the books would be handled and moved many times, a quick cleaning was all that was necessary on the upper floors. The basement had a thick layer of concrete dust, and each item needed to be handled separately. The special collections, which were fragile, also had to be cleaned.

In the basement, wet/dry vacuums were utilized with a hepa-filter on the nozzle. This was to prevent spreading the concrete dust out the back of the vacuum onto the floor again. Each book was removed from the shelf, then vacuumed, and the shelf was wiped down with a minimal amount of moisture. Then the books were returned to the dry shelves. The floors were cleaned several times a day to keep the dust down.

The special collections were cleaned by hand using dry chemical sponges to remove the fine layer of dust from each surface. This was time-consuming and potentially damaging to an already fragile collection. Each item was removed from the shelf and cleaned; then the shelves were wiped down and the collection returned to its place.

As a last measure, the air filters were all changed so the fine concrete dust that was trapped within would not blow loose again.

This renovation project was not completed when the concrete dust was discovered in and removed from the library. The following precautions were instituted, albeit late, to prevent additional damage to the collections. The plastic wall was replaced by a wooden wall and all cracks were sealed. The area between the dropped and true ceiling was covered to keep the dust out of the air-handling system. In addition, areas with missing ceiling tiles were sealed with plastic to prevent dust from settling onto the collections. When the sawing and renovation project was completed, the air-handling system was supposed to receive a cursory cleaning and the air filters were to be changed.

What Can We Learn?

The disaster could have been worse. Moisture would have changed the urgency of the situation and the type of cleanup necessary. *And* worst of all, the disaster could have been avoided in the first place. What do we learn from this crisis?

Proactive and preventive measures are extremely important. It is essential to impress this upon anyone starting a renovation or construction project in your building. Take the following five preventive steps:

1. Cover over and seal up areas that will allow access from the construction area to your collections.

2. Turn off the air-handling system to prevent the spread of dust and particulate matter, large and small.

3. Monitor the types of construction and make certain that safety precautions are being taken, such as no smoking and drinking in the area.

4. If possible, remove collections that could be damaged by the work. Photographic and audiovisual collections are particularly susceptible to damage from dust and particulate matter.

5. Plan for a thorough cleaning project when the renovation is completed.

Preservation and disaster response planning both involve a combination of proactive and reactive initiatives. When we consider all the factors that affect a building and the collections housed within, it is amazing that the materials have any projected life span. Maintaining a stable environment may be impossible during renovation and construction projects. However, protecting the collections from particulate matter and gross changes in the temperature and relative humidity are a must. Proactive and precautionary measures will help minimize the potential disaster.

Endnotes

1. Nick Artim, "*An Introduction to Fire Detection, Alarm, and Automatic Fire Sprinklers,*" Technical Leaflet—Emergency Management—Section 3 Leaflet 2, Northeast Document Conservation Center, 1999. Also at http://www.nedcc.org/plam3/tleaf32.htm.

2. Janice Stagnitto, "The Shrink Wrap Project at Rutgers University Special Collections and Archives," *AIC Book and Paper Group Annual*, 1993, v.12, p. 56–60. Reprinted in *Abby Newsletter* 18, no. 4–5 (August–September 1994); also available at http://palimpsest.stanford.edu/byorg/abbey/an/an18/an18-4/an18-411.html.

3. Originally published in *MAC Newsletter*, June 1996. For an article on the same disaster, see Barbra Buckner Higginbotham, "Practical Preservation Projects Managing Emergencies: Small Construction Projects," *Technicalities* 16, no. 9 (October 1996): 1, 12–14.

Planning

The *planning* phase is where everything is supposed to come together on paper. The more forethought and preparation for disasters, the better the response to the news that a disaster has occurred. The building survey is completed and necessary repairs made. Vulnerable collections are identified and floor plans are drawn. Now is the time to assign responsibilities for activating and implementing the disaster response plan, designate priorities for recovery of collections, and review the insurance and financial position for recovery of materials if they are damaged. Very small or one-person libraries, archives, and historical societies should enlist the assistance of others in their community to help create and activate a plan to recover the operations and collections of the institution.

Elements of a Disaster Response Plan

The following list outlines the four phases of a disaster response plan: prevention, planning, response, and recovery. Use it to make certain all the components are accounted for.

Add to this list or modify it to reflect the needs of your institution *and* your specific disaster response plan. Use it as the table of contents for your plan. Just add page numbers to each section or category.

Make a basic response plan with phone numbers the first page of your disaster response manual for easy reference and contact. Post the daytime numbers for the disaster response team at phones for a swift response (see figure 4.1).

For a quick and dirty plan, use the following three response phases in conjunction with the seven steps in the introduction.

Prevention

- Survey the building and collection for potential damage and hazards. Check fire, smoke, and door alarms and exit signs.

- Mark collections that are water or heat sensitive. Make certain they are stored in areas that have the least potential for destruction.

- Monitor indoor air quality.

FIGURE 4.1. Disaster Response Team Contact Information

Name	Phone

Emergency Meeting Place is located at

_____

Alternative Operating Location

Street address: _____

Contact name and phone number: _____

Directions (or append map): _____

- Examine remote storage facilities.
- Plan for construction and renovation projects.
- Create a list of consultants and conservators who can deal with the damaged format (get alternative names).

Planning

- Select the disaster response team and alternative staff members.
- Assign responsibilities for each of the response phases.
- Set priorities for recovery of each of the collections (by format, type, department, floor, or building).
- Plan for large, small, and wide-area disasters.
- Plan for damage to computers.
- Review insurance coverage and update as needed. Determine what is not covered and time, situation, and money limitations. Set an update schedule for annual review.
- Establish a communications policy.
- Contact disaster response companies and consultants for a walk-through and discussion of their roles in potential disasters.
- Work with facilities and security staff to discuss their roles during a potential disaster.
- Train the disaster response team and explain responsibilities to the rest of the staff.
- Practice response phases, evaluate plan, and revise.

Response (3 phases)

1. Respond to notification of the disaster.
   - Gather the team.
   - Alert outside professionals of the disaster.
   - Determine if the building should be closed and for how long.
2. Assess the situation and damage.
   - Call in outside assistance.
   - Organize recovery steps based upon prioritization (developed or assigned in the planning phase).
   - Set up communications—internal and external.
3. Begin to rescue and recover collections.
   - Reassign/reallocate staff as needed.
   - Deal with emotional issues.

Recovery

- Restore primary services (skeleton staff).
- Restore primary functions (skeleton functions with available staff).
- Return to normal (most staff back to regular duties).
- Evaluate response procedures and revise the disaster response plan.

Disaster Response Team

A disaster response team is essential for the smooth execution of the disaster response operation. Members of the team should be capable of executing the plan and performing the tasks. They should be trained in techniques to recover water-damaged materials and be familiar with recovery priorities.

Most disaster response teams consist of four to six people, with several backup persons to call in an emergency. Ideally, the team should be headed by the person in charge of preservation or data management. In some instances, all the members of the preservation or Information Systems (IS) departments are the team. Other members of the team should be selected from the professional and paraprofessional staff. If there are several departments or locations, designate a team for each. In the case of a smaller library, a representative from the building's facilities maintenance department should be on the team.

The disaster response team is the first to be called to the disaster site. They will assess the scope of the disaster, the tasks that must be accomplished, and the number of personnel necessary to complete the recovery operation.

Roles and Responsibilities

For a disaster response plan to be effective and to avoid several people dealing with the same problem at once, assign responsibilities to the members of the disaster response team, the library director, and other staff and personnel. It is important to have a second person as a backup for each of the responsibilities in case a team member is out of town or unavailable. Some responsibilities fall naturally into the domains of team members and staff, such as assigning the IS librarian (the one in charge of the computer systems) the responsibility of dealing with computer problems and issues and ordering cleaning and replacement of damaged equipment and software.

Disaster response team members should be able to deal with the responsibilities assigned them and be capable of making decisions concerning how to carry out the associated duties. In some cases, the responsibility will require the team member to contact consultants and contractors or purchase supplies and minor pieces of equipment. The person assigned that responsibility must have the designated fiscal authority to do so. If necessary, the disaster response team should set up criteria to follow before exercising this type of emergency fiscal authority.

The responsibilities and roles for disaster response team members may be assigned in phases to correspond with the different aspects of disaster response: immediate response, assessment, and recovery. Preassignment of responsibilities is important so that the disaster response team knows what to expect of their energies and time from the minute they are informed of the disaster until the situation has returned to "normal."

Director: The library director and the deputy director, if the library is large enough, deal with the administration or board of trustees or governing board. Except for one-person libraries, the director should not head the disaster response team because, in addition to the duties of running the library, the director's job and responsibility are to be the chief administrator of the institution. Once the disaster is declared, the director must make informed major decisions and allocate funds and extra staff to assist with the response and recovery phases of disaster response. In most cases, the library will be insured for some of the loss or will have funds set aside for such an emergency.

The director may deal directly with the insurance agent and adjuster or designate that responsibility. Make certain that the designee is familiar with the insurance policy and has the authority to contact the insurance company.

In addition, the director may wish to work with consultants and disaster response/drying companies directly or assign those responsibilities to the disaster response team leader. In either case, it is helpful if the consultants and disaster response companies are familiar with the workings of the institution, the staff, and the recovery priorities. The director's involvement in the disaster response plan is crucial to boost morale both during and after the disaster. The director might provide food, drink, and rest periods or may assign that responsibility to the disaster response team leader.

Regardless of how involved the library director is in the disaster response and recovery phases, there should be regular meetings of the disaster response team and the director and regular updates for other staff about overall recovery of the institution.

Chief Financial Officer: If the institution is large enough to have a fiscal officer, then the director may need to go to this administrator to request emergency allocation of financial resources. This officer may handle the insurance policy, or it might be under the domain of the risk management office. During the planning phase, identify who to go to for emergency funding and for initiating insurance claims. If the disaster is small, it may merely require the director to allocate emergency funds from the budget to cover the disaster recovery expenses.

Team Leader: The team leader coordinates response and recovery operations; works with team members; communicates with the director, team, members, and the public information officer (PIO); coordinates volunteer efforts; and arranges for multiple shifts. The director may ask the team leader to assign rest breaks and provide frequent updates about the overall situation to the team and the staff. The team leader either arranges for a temporary work location or assigns a team member to do so, and assists team members with their designated responsibilities (see a list of jobs to assign on p. 43). The team leader lets staff know where to report and for which shift.

Team Members: The disaster response team members lead efforts in designated tasks from the team leader and wherever else needed, such as supervising the move to a temporary location and arranging for phone connections, equipment, and temporary staff. They train staff and volunteers, locate additional supplies, and communicate with the team leader on a regular basis.

Public Information Officer (PIO)/Communications Officer: As the institution's official spokesperson, the PIO communicates with the media by writing and sending press releases to television and radio stations and the newspapers as to the situation, temporary hours, and services. The PIO also releases contact information to vendors, suppliers, and patrons.

Information Systems (IS) Librarian: The IS librarian gets data and computers up and running. This may include the stand-alone PCs, CD-ROM towers, LANs, and other networked computer systems and their associated peripherals. The online public access catalog (OPAC) may or may not fall under the domain of the IS librarian; the same is true of the website and digital resources. If the IS librarian is not responsible for the library's computer systems, then the main computing staff or IS department should be involved in getting the public access terminals and their associated programs and data up and running. Don't forget to involve the IS department in the library's disaster response plan process so that they know when they might be called upon and the disaster response team knows what the IS department can do for them.

Administration: The administrator allocates emergency and contingency funds, approves hiring of disaster recovery firms, meets with insurance adjusters, works with the overall plan, etc. The administrator should arrange one or two meetings with department heads about the disaster response actions and progress.

Security: In the event of a disaster, triggered alarm, water leaks, or broken pipes, security staff should notify the disaster response team. Security should help prevent theft and notify the library/archives about broken windows and doors. If there is no security department, or it is small, then hire temporary security staff for the duration of the disaster response and recovery phases. Security should have keys to all the rooms in the building.

Facilities Maintenance: The facilities maintenance staff should clean up water, fire damage, and debris; board up broken windows and doors; and help with miscellaneous cleanup efforts. It may fall under their domain to hire a disaster response/drying company based upon the library/archives' recommendation. They should know the location of all utility shutoff valves and how to shut them off.

Consultants: A consultant should be able to recommend treatment options and write specifications for drying the collection and the building. He or she should help coordinate response efforts and locate necessary resources, supplies, and services. Consultants should help train staff and volunteers; explain options for recovery; and serve as liaison with the director, administration, team leader, and the insurance company, if requested. Consultants can direct facilities maintenance staff efforts if no drying company is contracted with. A good consultant can identify and locate additional contractors in "hazardous" situations and should know conservators and specialists who can work with your collections. In some cases, consultants may be asked to direct or lead response and recovery efforts.

Disaster Response/Drying Companies: These companies dry and "recover" all wet materials, furnishings, and the building. They should provide the best possible treatment based on specifications for "recovery." A disaster response/drying company should return all treated items in the best possible condition, having removed all mold, dirt, mud, etc. after drying the materials. A disaster response/drying company may be called in by the consultant, the insurance adjuster, or the institution. On the other hand, some disaster response/drying companies regularly contract with preservation consultants for work with cultural institutions. If your institution is insured, the drying and recovery of the collection is usually covered by the insurance policy.

Risk Manager—Insurance Agent: She or he evaluates the level of insurance needed and should be able to identify potential risks and hazards to the collections.

Now that we have discussed what each of the various roles entails, let's look at the tasks necessary to quickly and efficiently respond to a disaster and deal with the damage.

All or some of these jobs will need to be done during the response phase. Designate the appropriate disaster response team members to perform these tasks or make these decisions during a disaster or ahead of time.

- Contact the director.
- Assess the damage.
- Determine if the building needs to be closed and for how long.
- Contact outside assistance, including a consultant and a disaster response/drying company.
- Arrange for security and maintenance to secure the premises.
- Contact an insurance agent and assess the status of contingency funds.
- Organize the staff to perform "duties as assigned."
- Determine if the work needs to be done in shifts.
- Decide if volunteers are needed and where to use them.
- Have standing water removed and humidity decreased.
- Check equipment (computers and peripherals, photocopiers, etc.) for damage, and arrange for drying, cleaning, and recertification. Don't forget to check diskettes and tape for damage and arrange for cleaning, etc., when computer equipment is ready for use; then check the functionality of the operating system, software, and data. Restore data and operations as required.
- Order supplies for packing boxes of water-damaged books and other media.
- Arrange for shipping and freezing of water-damaged items, as appropriate.
- Supervise packing of boxes whether done by staff, volunteers, or disaster response/drying company's staff.
- Arrange for an alternative location from which to operate.
- Send press releases to the media. Inform patrons, suppliers, and vendors about hours, address, and phone number.

- Monitor the building for mold, increased relative humidity and temperatures, and other environmental problems such as excess dust, debris, and soot.
- Arrange for breaks, food, and drink.

Lists to Create and Update during the Planning Phase

As part of the planning phase, designate the following jobs to specific disaster response team members:

- Identify suppliers of packing and shipping products and services, including a lumber supply store and a freezer storage facility.
- Identify and contact preservation consultants who specialize in, or have actual experience with, disaster response. Put them on the contact list.
- Contact local and regional disaster response drying companies. Put them on the contact list.
- Designate a place to meet if the building is damaged or inaccessible.
- Identify temporary office space for administration and non-public services work. If there is a lot of office space in your community, then note where to find it and how to contact the rental agencies. Also identify temporary work space in a nearby community.
- Make a note of the local cellular phone and office equipment rental companies in your community and a nearby community.
- Identify local security companies.
- Designate a team member to review the insurance policy yearly.
- Designate one or two team members to be responsible for updating the building survey and prioritization for recovery decisions yearly.
- Put together or purchase a basic disaster response kit (see ProText, Inc., p. 136).
- Find out who is responsible for stocking and maintaining the first aid kits. Check them regularly.

- Place this information and the contact lists in the back of the plan.
- Ensure that the disaster response team leader distributes the plan, in draft and final forms, to the disaster response team members and facilities maintenance and security departments. All versions should be distributed to every department. The disaster response team members should keep a copy of the most up-to-date plan at home or in their cars in case the building is inaccessible or the disaster happens at night.

Now that responsibilities during the planning and response phases have been assigned, the disaster response team begins planning for response and recovery of collections.

Prioritization for Recovery

One of the most difficult phases of the planning process is prioritizing the collection for recovery in the event of a disaster. The disaster response team has already identified vulnerable collections. Now each department and institution must make decisions that are specific for their collections, mission statements, and services to patrons and clients.

Prioritization requires looking at subject areas of the collection as a whole in an attempt to determine in what order items should be rescued and recovered should they be damaged in a disaster. It is the difficult matter of trying to save the most important of the most important items in the collection. This process looks at the core collection for unique, irreplaceable items. Are they shelved together? Are the items most vulnerable to water stored away from overhead water pipes, safe from vicarious disasters? Or is everything shelved together? In the second phase of the prioritization process, examine how each department's collection fits into the mission of the institution as a whole. In the case of a large scale disaster, where the entire building is affected, the disaster response team will have to know which departments are more crucial to the mission of the institution to rescue the rescuable.

Determining the priorities of recovery also provides an opportunity to consider future collection development projects. For example, if the subject indexes are damaged, would the institution replace them with such electronic formats as CD-ROMs or interactive databases? Or if paper issues of periodicals are affected, do you know the overlap of the microfilm collection with print periodicals? Would the institution replace paper copies with microfilm? Is there money to do this? Or would the department institute document delivery for the issues where the hard copy was destroyed and there is no microfilm? Or are some of the periodicals available on the Internet, either for free or with a subscription? If the answer is yes to any of these questions, then the priority level can be the lowest, with the collection development decision to discard and update with the newest format.

During the prioritization phase, departments might initiate overdue weeding projects, because a disaster is not the time to weed the collection. Recovering the damaged items and rescuing the undamaged are primary concerns. In the same vein, a disaster does not mean the institution will get a completely new collection. Not only is this impractical, but very few, if any, institutions have the insurance to cover the cost of purchasing an entire collection. The only time an institution may have the opportunity to purchase a new collection is if the building burned to the ground; *however*, insurance still would not be enough to replace every lost volume.

After the collection has been surveyed and prioritization for recovery decisions made, the areas of each department or floor should be clearly marked to identify the different levels of prioritization. Remember that this cannot be an item-by-item prioritization, but one by area or type of collection.

Indicate the levels of prioritization for recovery on the floor plan for each department or floor. This step is important, for during a disaster, it can be very chaotic, with collections in disarray. Also, the collection may be packed out for recovery or storage by a disaster response company, whose personnel cannot and should not make these decisions for your institution.

All the prioritization for recovery decisions should be made during the *planning phase*, while staff is in a rational state of mind and emotions are stable. At this time (before the disaster), staff who are emotionally connected to the collections can make informed choices about the future of the collections and the institution.

If prioritization decisions are not made ahead of time, they will have to be made "on the fly," under the following situations:

- While awaiting permission to enter the building

- While looking at water-damaged areas

- By an outside consultant who works with the library, the insurance company, or the disaster response company. Although a consultant may be familiar with the workings and basic needs of cultural institutions, he or she may not know the collection development policy or mission statement of your institution. If the outside consultant is a librarian, then ask for solid, unemotional suggestions for the staff to work from. An overview of the institution's mission statement and collection development policies is in order. If you intend to use an outside consultant, it is best to meet during the planning phase, describe policies and missions ahead of time, and acquaint the consultant with the building and collection layout. In fact, if an outside consultant is prearranged, then write the consultant into the plan and place contact information in the primary response phase.

- By the disaster response firm while packing out the collection. Remember that the disaster response firm may have no experience with libraries, archives, or museums. Suggestions from the disaster response firm for recovery and removal of collections may be random and uninformed, especially if there has been no prior contact between the firm and the institution or the disaster response team.

In the first two scenarios above, prioritization for recovery decisions is made while emotions are high, and decisions may not be in the best interest of the collection or institution's mission as a whole. It is important to review prioritization decisions

- at least once a year;

- whenever a new collection is added;

- when the mission statement is reviewed or changed;

- when new services are offered, especially those key to servicing patrons;

- when a department is added or subtracted or if a floor, wing, or building is added or subtracted; and

- if a major shift in the shelving of the collection affects the floor plan.

At this point, it is important to revise

- the floor plan and

- the prioritization for recovery list.

The disaster response team should work with department heads and building administrators to prioritize the paper-based collections; non-print and non-paper collections, including photographs and audiovisual (AV) materials; computers and their associated magnetic media; and office, administrative, and institutional records, per the records-retention schedule.

Prioritization Categories

Prioritization decisions fit into five basic categories:

1. Irreparably damaged or irreplaceable due to format or value

2. Essential to the mission of the institution or to provide basic services to patrons

3. Important to round out the basic collections or services

4. Nice to have but not essential to the primary mission of the institution

5. Can be discarded because they are replaced on a regular basis (usually standing orders and serials)

Office and business records fall within the third category. Computers, peripheral equipment, software, and data may fall in category 2 or 3 depending upon the type of institution and its dependence upon computerized services.

Category 1 includes all those items that are irreparably damaged by water or excess temperatures and those items that are irreplaceable such as "rare books" and reference tools that are crucial to the mission of the institution and are also out of print. These items include photographs on glass plates, nitrate film, and the various processes that react poorly to water, thereby destroying the image. In the case of glass plate negatives and some other formats, the adhesive in the bonding layer releases from the base and the image slides off the support. Nitrate film reacts violently with water and so should be stored away from any chance of water damage. It should be disposed of appropriately as it is considered a "hazardous waste."

In the case of water-sensitive photographs, mark their containers in such a way as to identify them at a glance. Mark them with a special color or label, so they can be removed quickly and boxed again if necessary. Mark heavy boxed collections for handling with caution as they may be damaged if dropped. This is very important when using temporary or hired labor.

Magnetic tape can be irreparably damaged by excessive temperatures. Tape begins to melt at 125° Fahrenheit. Magnetic media can withstand the ravages of water for a short period of time, but they should be removed from water as quickly as possible and sent to an appropriate vendor for drying and copying. *Do not freeze magnetic media.*

Category 2 includes those items that are essential to the mission of the institution. The staff of the institution cannot provide basic, key services to patrons or clients without these items. Category 2 recovery decisions can be based upon collection development policy and overall mission statements or upon the mission and focus of each department or building. For example, if the institution has a special architecture reference department where the focus is on the history of architecture, it might contain various formats and media but also unusual reference materials to answer specialized questions. If so, the entire department might be designated for removal and recovery as quickly as possible. Other types of collections that fall within this category are special ready-reference items that are not part of the standing order system.

Category 3 items are important to round out the basic core collections or services. These mate-

rials flesh out the different departments and services, creating the identity of the institution as a whole. These also include the rest of the special collections materials, less-rare "rare books," and the archives. Within this category are the records created by offices and the business and financial records of the institution. Priorities for recovery, discard, and destruction of business records should be based upon the records-retention schedule established by the records manager of the institution. If there is no records-retention manager, then consult a specialist and place the core retention schedule in the disaster response plan.

Note that business, office, and financial records that are held within the archives and special collections department are *not* the same as an archives collection, which is a unique collection of documents. Although the office and business records may fall under the jurisdiction of the institution's archivist, they should not be treated the same.

The following are some basic rules of thumb for the archives:

- Papers that comprise the legal history of the institution are considered permanent records and must be retained for the life of the institution. These are a top priority for recovery.

- Business and financial records may be considered permanent depending upon their content; otherwise, follow the records-retention schedule.

- Office files are usually not considered permanent records and should follow the records-retention schedule.

Other options for archival records are microfilming after a designated period of time and destroying the paper records. If the damaged records have been filmed, and the film is stored in a safe location, then discard and destroy those archival records.

Category 4 includes all materials that are nice to have but are not essential to the primary mission of the institution. These items may prompt the question, "Why do we have these in the first place?"

Category 5 is materials that can be discarded because they are regularly replaced via the following mechanisms: standing orders (directories, basic reference tools); annual or regular replacements (almanacs, encyclopedias); or CD-ROMs, microfilm, or online interactive databases. The last category may be supplemented by document delivery services, especially if the damaged collection included an extensive number of periodicals.

Prioritization for Recovery of Computers

Prioritization for recovery of computers, peripherals, software, and data varies depending upon the mission and services of the institution or the department.

- **Computers and Peripherals:** These can be dried, cleaned, and recertified if they are not damaged by excessive temperatures. If they are damaged, the prioritization statement may be the same as for periodicals: consider the age and replace if old or recover if new after checking on the scope of insurance coverage.

- **Software:** If it is unique or obsolete, the software must be recovered. This type of software should be backed up on a regular basis and stored in an off-site location. Any changes to the program should be backed up immediately and should replace the tape in the off-site storage area. Check to see if this falls within the domain of the IS department of the institution as a whole and how their disaster response plan fits with the library/archives. Some recent studies show that software programs won't read versions more than three generations old. So libraries should be upgrading software within three generations or five years.[1]

- **Data and Information:** Data should be backed up regularly if created on-site. If it comes to the institution on a regular basis, such as CD-ROMs or magnetic tape databases, then load the older information and wait for the new data.

- **OPAC (Online Public Access Catalog):** This should be backed up regularly. Contact the service provider or vendor to determine if backup is done on a regular basis and who is responsible for reloading the data should the system crash or the hardware fail. Ask who provides the temporary hardware. This should be discussed with the IS department to determine under whose domain this service falls and who will contact the service provider. Make certain to write the appropriate contact information in the primary/secondary phase of the response plan.

- **Website:** The website should be updated regularly and copies of the current layout and format should be stored off-site. If the library's servers host the website, then care should be taken to backup regularly. If the website is located on a remote server, find out what their backup and disaster response plans are and back up accordingly. If the remote server crashes and your site is destroyed, you will have to reinstall or remount from your most recent backup.

Recovery of personal office files depends upon the needs of the individual. Items the individual might wish to rescue include a Rolodex or personal and professional contact file, personal diskettes, unique projects, and research materials. Personal office files are not usually part of category 1 recovery materials or in the first wave of pack out and removal. Provide time for staff members to clean out their personal areas after the primary affected areas are dealt with.

Difficult prioritization for recovery decisions includes periodicals in hard copy or paper form. They are often available in other formats, including microfilm and microfiche. Other formats, such as on CD-ROM or via a document delivery service, may be as cost-effective as purchasing paper retrospective collections. Today, periodicals and journals are often available full-text on the Internet via subscription services or on-site licensing agreements. Take a look at your periodical holdings and see if this is an option for your library or archive. The other aspect of the retrospective periodical collection to consider is the type of paper. If the periodicals are printed on clay-coated paper, it may be difficult or impossible to rescue these items from water before they are irreparably damaged.

It is important to remember when acting on the prioritization for recovery decisions that if the items are not damaged or in danger of damage, then keep the materials safe. Prioritization for recovery only pertains to collections and departments that are damaged.

Planning for Small, Large, and Wide-Area Disasters

As discussed in section 1, there are three sizes of disaster to consider when designing the disaster response phase of the plan: small, or localized; large; and wide area. Every size of disaster involves the same basic procedures. If you have a large scale or wide-area disaster, then adjust your plan to accommodate the loss of building, infrastructure, and external support. You may also have to look outside your community for assistance or a temporary location.

Small scale disasters affect a department, floor, or collection. This type of disaster could be caused by a water pipe break, leaking roof, isolated flooding from below, an isolated fire, or a mold infection. It may require closing the building or department until the situation is under control or merely suspending the localized services.

Large scale disasters affect the building or institution as a whole but are "defined" disasters, with community resources available. This type of disaster, usually caused by fire or a large water main break, often requires closing the building or interrupting services for one to two days.

Wide-area disasters are usually caused by natural disasters (earthquakes, tornadoes, hurricanes, or huge forest fires) that affect the infrastructure of the city or a large geographical area. In the wake of the destruction of the World Trade Center and damage to the Pentagon, we have learned many lessons about the impact of wide-area disasters on the infrastructure of cities and businesses. These disasters will affect the personal lives of the staff. Community resources and those of the surrounding area are stretched to provide for all affected businesses. The building or institution will be closed until at least the infrastructure is restored. Seek assistance and services from beyond the affected area.

Many institutions plan for large scale and wide-area disasters. These types of disasters may happen in the life of an institution, maybe even more than once, as in the case of the World Trade Center.

Start your response plan by considering the occurrence of small scale disasters. They are fairly common and are encountered on a routine basis, maybe even once or twice a year, depending upon the condition and maintenance of the building. Sometimes they occur as closely spaced events. In this case, willing and enthusiastic participation in response and recovery activities will decrease as the disasters increase in frequency. If the scope of damage is small enough, response may require only the disaster response team and the members of the affected department.

Because small disasters are more common, response and recovery decisions are easier to define and decide upon. Lack of preparedness for small disasters can create larger disasters and ultimately affect the entire building or department.

Large scale disasters affect large portions of the building or the entire building. This scale disaster will require the disaster response team and additional staff to deal with containment and recovery. The best way to deal with this type of disaster is to close the building until everything is under control. Service will definitely be affected and may require relocating the most severely damaged departments. The disaster response team will also need to deal with emotional issues because whole portions of the collection may be damaged or destroyed. In this case, it might be useful to ask for outside assistance, such as a consultant, for one or two days to help assess the damage, make decisions about recovery and vendor selection, and act with the disaster response team leader as liaison between staff, administration, and the outside vendors. The consultant can provide additional or specialized training and education to the rest of the staff if necessary.

In a wide-area disaster caused by weather, the infrastructure of the institution or the city is affected. Ask for outside assistance immediately, preferably from outside the affected area. Contact vendors of services from outside the affected area. Outside assistance is imperative in this case because they are not emotionally tied to the collection or institution; their families and homes were not damaged; and they should be able to draw supplies and services from far outside the affected area.

A wide-area disaster may require waiting to activate the response plan until the basic infrastructure is in place. However, evidence of a written response plan *could* hasten permission to enter the building to begin recovery of affected and damaged collections, especially if no water or power is needed.

Coordination of recovery during a wide-area disaster is more difficult than during the other types of disasters because work must be done within the constraints of no infrastructure and a heavy demand upon resources in the immediate and surrounding communities. There may be a shortage of trucks, storage space, supplies, temporary help, and temporary working space. Select at least one of each type of contractual service from outside the immediate geographical area of the institution. Remember that cellular phones will be heavily relied upon during wide-area disasters, causing delays in communication. On September 11, 2001, some institutions and individuals had great luck with pagers that can receive e-mail. Perhaps this will be an acceptable alternative to cellular phones.

A large scale disaster could be long term and just as devastating as a wide-area disaster if caused by an outage of power or phones. If the institution is small or provides time-dependent services, this type of outage could destroy the business. Consider options of working from a remote location. Disasters caused by power and telecommunications outages will become more common and more devastating as libraries, archives, and museums become even more dependent upon technology to provide even the most basic of services. A backup power and telecommunications system is especially important for access to computer and automated services.

Planning for Damage to Computers and Automated Services

The focus of this publication is planning for disasters caused by water and fire, not computer crashes. However, with the prevalence of comput-

ers in almost every facet of library and archives services, for public use and behind-the-scenes operations, it is necessary to plan for the loss of computer access.

There are usually two or three types of computer services in libraries, historical societies, and archives:

- public catalogs and circulation systems, and Internet resources;
- LANs and networked public access to CD-ROM and tape-loaded databases, and fee-based access to digital collections; and
- internal databases and networked and stand-alone PCs used for administrative and fiscal purposes.

Most large institutions have both an Information Services department for computers institution-wide and a staff member in the library/archives responsible for the computers in the building. The internal staff member usually deals with computers running the OPAC, circulation system, cataloging functions, and other data services.

In the planning phase, just as you established priorities for recovery of print and non-paper collections, it is important to decide which computer services and systems must be restored first when a disaster happens. In the case of computers, three types of disasters could occur: fire and water damage, power outages, and telecommunications outages.

Look at the services the library/archives provides that rely on computers. Discuss how the institution will function without these services and for how long. Is the institution so dependent upon computer services that operation from an alternative location or dial-up access is essential? This is often true of corporate and special libraries. As traditional libraries are increasingly dependent upon computers, alternative operation locations are more necessary.

Primary Recovery: Public Catalog and Circulation Systems, and Perhaps the Website: Determine how long the library/archives can function before lack of an automated circulation system will cripple public services. How far behind can your institution be? Is there a portable, battery-operated, or smaller backup system that can be utilized in the meantime? And for how long?

In terms of the public catalog, is there another way to access the institution's holdings, such as a printed subject access catalog with associated call numbers? Is the staff able to use that method of access effectively enough to have the building open when the computers are down for a long period of time? And for how long? If the answer to the last question is indefinitely *and* the circulation functions are separate from the catalog, the OPAC does not belong in the primary recovery category but in the second or third. The OPAC should then come up at the same time as cataloging.

Determine what lack of access to the website and its associated services means to the library and its patrons. Can the students and faculty access the digital collections of texts and journals through another computer or are the OPAC and website interdependent? If the website is integrated into the OPAC or the circulation system, then it needs to come up at the same time; if not, then the website can wait and be categorized as a secondary priority. Of course, if the website is housed on a separate system, which may be preferable, then the plan should be modified accordingly.

Secondary Recovery: LANs and Networked Public Access to CD-ROM and Tape-Loaded Databases: Can the library/archives provide services without these products, and for how long? What about dial-up access? Is the library/archives willing to offer dial-up access to patrons, and for how long? If these services provide full-text access to journals that are not held by the institution, are there provisions to offer document delivery? At what cost, and who pays the cost? Is this an alternative if the periodical collection is damaged?

Tertiary Recovery: Internal Databases and Networked and Stand-alone PCs Used for Administration and Fiscal Purposes: Where do you rank fiscal and payroll services in the prioritization for recovery of computer operations? If payroll and fiscal services are contracted out, does that company have a backup or disaster response plan? If payroll is internal, how will the institution pay the staff while the fiscal computer system is down? Where is the backup tape, and how old is it? Con-

firm that the business interruption or extra expense rider of your policy will assist with payroll.

What other services are available online or via computers? How long can the institution do without them? What are your options? Determine which of these services fits into what recovery category.

Just as you have made decisions to replace print indexes with CD-ROM and online databases, is there an option to upgrade to a new system altogether that provides better access, coverage, or response time?

After determining the order to restore computer-based services, the next step is to create a list of the types and locations of hardware and software in the building. This will make it easier to identify the damaged and lost items for recovery or replacement.

Inventory each department, system, or floor, depending upon how the equipment and software is distributed. Note if the software is on a LAN. What is the serial number? Is there a licensing agreement, etc.? Do the same thing for hardware, noting the configuration of the peripherals. Put together simple instructions for rebooting the system and loading data from tape backups.

This information will be necessary for replacing the lost and damaged computer equipment and software. The insurance company will want a list of the damaged items.

In terms of software, unlike publishers and book jobbers who may have a plan to lower prices or lease books in the event of a disaster, software companies may require the purchase of new software and licenses. If this is the case, will your data run on updated versions of the software? The rule of thumb is that after three software generations, you may not be able to convert forward. In any case, you can never read backwards; that is, if you have data in version 4 and you are using version 6 or 7 it is readable. But if you save the data with version 7, you will *not* be able to read it with version 4. It is very important that you continue to update the software that is in storage and used for backups so all data can be read.

It is important to keep in mind that both the hardware and software can be recovered if water damaged. It is lack of access to the information that compounds the crisis.

Technology

Increased dependence of libraries and archives on computers, data, databases and telecommunications, websites, e-mail, and other technological advances requires increased diligence to disaster response and contingency plans. This part of the plan should both stand alone and be integrated into the plan for the library/archives.

During the planning and prevention stage, determine where in the list of priorities, computer and Information Systems (IS) functions fall. The most important functions need to be back up and running right away. Statistics show that for every hour of lost data it will take a day to re-input it; and for every day lost, a week, during the course of a normal work load.

For most libraries, the most important computer function to restore first is the circulation system. This way books can be checked out and returned. Just think about how many books come back in the course of a normal workday. How much time will it take for you to check them all in? You will also need to decide what your policy will be for circulating materials without the computers. Do you write down all the barcode numbers by hand? How long will that take to input?

The library's second priority for getting computers up is probably the catalog so that reference functions can be restored. It will be important to determine how the website for the library and its online catalog are integrated with the catalog used by staff. If they are one and the same, how long can the website be down before you lose patrons?

During the planning phase, another important question is who hosts the website for your library? Is it in the same physical location as the main library or is it someplace separate? If the first, then how will IS maintain the website and its functions when access to the building is restricted? If the website is hosted on another computer or in another location, then determine what type of disaster response/contingency plan they have.

Next, a solid review and test of the daily backup procedures is very important. More than one person

should know how to back up the information, databases, and websites. All backup tapes must be stored off-site, whether in the trunk of your car, your house or a data vault, or all three. Clear, simple instructions should be posted so that anyone could back up and take down the system in an emergency. Make certain that the UPS (Universal Power Supply) is rated to last as long as the shut down procedure takes.

Part of planning is testing to make certain that people know what to do in an emergency. Thus it is important to test the backup tapes to make certain they work. It is also important to test how long various restore procedures take, and that more than one person knows how to perform partial and full restoration of software and hardware. Make certain the instructions for this procedure are clear and simple.

Test the full restoration of your system, which should include the operating system, the software, and the data. Know the hardware configurations and requirements as well as the software systems necessary to rebuild the system. This is incredibly important if your library is using obsolete or proprietary software and hardware. Make certain you have current copies of all changes to software and hardware needs stored with the backup tapes.

It is essential that two or more people be familiar with your hardware and software needs. Undoubtedly one of them will be on vacation when the crisis occurs.

When planning and practicing your plan for restoration of computer functions in the library, review the frequency of backups, where they are stored, how long it takes to get the backup tapes to whatever location you are at, and how many hours a full restoration of systems will take. (Reloading all your software on a personal computer can take more than four hours.) Be certain to document all this in the appendix of your plan.

During the response and recovery phase of your disaster, you will need to assess the damage to hardware and software. Document which pieces of hardware need to be cleaned and recertified, and which will need to be replaced. A careful review of the computer rider in your insurance plan will provide monetary guidelines for how much they will pay for operation at a temporary or remote location, and for how long. Depending upon how badly the building that houses the computer systems is damaged, you may need to find an alternative location to operate from. This is the location where the hardware and software will be set up. Don't forget to tell the company that stores your backup tapes where you are located and how to access the building. At the same time, you may need to arrange for telecommunications access from the computers to the library or your server.

During the recovery phase of your disaster, the IS department will need to retrieve the backup tapes, and determine where they will be operating from. It may be easiest to operate from a remote location temporarily, to be out of the way of the disaster response companies that are cleaning, deodorizing, and restoring the library. The recovery phase is not the time to have to purchase new software and install it only to find out that it doesn't work with the data.

As the library comes back to some sense of normalcy, the IS department will need to reintegrate the computer functions. After the crisis is over, it is time to evaluate what changes need to be made in terms of procedures, hardware and software, and priorities.

Insurance

Reviewing the insurance policy enables the institution to respond quickly, thereby limiting the damage to the collections. There are some important things to keep in mind about insurance policies. When a disaster occurs and there is enough damage to warrant calling the insurance company, let them know what happened. You do not have to wait for an adjuster to arrive to either activate the plan or begin to recover the collections. Document the damage with photographs and memos or checklists before starting any recovery efforts. After reviewing the insurance policy, you will know how much your deductible is (that is, how much the institution pays out of the contingency fund before the insurance kicks in).

Libraries, archives, and historical societies have a number of different types of insurance coverage and internal funding constraints. Many institutions are insured, but it is not uncommon for the policies to have a large deductible. The smaller the institu-

tion, the more likely it is to have insurance with a manageable deductible. Individual items may be underinsured and undervalued. Insurance for the structure may be adequate or not, depending upon the age of the building and the financial status of the institution. Insurance riders for "recovery services" and business interruption may be present; if so, there is a ceiling on the recovery amount after the deductible. The library should create a contingency fund that covers the deductible. Find out if the signature of the financial officer for the entire institution is needed before expenditures are permitted. If the job needs to go out for bid, hope that there is an emergency provision at your institution for fast bids and preliminary allocation of funds. Contact the facilities maintenance department and find out what is covered under their contingency funds for repairs, outside services, and general consulting.

It is not unusual for public institutions—those funded by state, city, county, and federal agencies—to be self-insured. This means that the institution must pay from its own funds. Some public institutions may be covered under the county's or city's insurance. If the institution is self-insured, funds may need to be legislated to be able to afford recovery from a large scale or wide-area disaster. That means a bill would have to be drawn up and voted upon for allocation of state, county, or city funds unless there is an emergency executive order for release of funds or an official emergency is declared. If the latter is the case, the Federal Emergency Management Agency (FEMA) comes into play (state or federal). The institution usually has to lay out the funds, or at least contract the work, and then be reimbursed by FEMA. Corporate libraries and information and records centers are usually insured under the corporate insurance policy.

Aspects of an Insurance Policy
Building or Structure

It is essential to have insurance that covers the loss of a building or structure so that the building can be reconstructed after a fire or total disaster. If the building is not a total loss, the insurance should pay for the drying and recovery of the walls, floors, ceilings, and the mechanical equipment in the building.

If the business, library, or information center is located in rented space, the insurance policy should cover recovery, cleaning, and reconstruction of the area. Do not assume that the building owner's insurance will cover the damage within rented space. In fact, if the damage is the result of negligence on the part of the renter, such as broken water pipes from turning the heat too low, the renter may be responsible for all the damage.

If the property is jointly owned or owned by a government agency, determine—ahead of time—who pays for damage and loss.

Make certain that the insurance is adequate to cover potential hazards. If the building is in an active earthquake or flood zone, determine if the insurance will cover these potential hazards. If not, arrange for adequate coverage.

With the increase in the number of claims for mold damage and removal or remediation, some insurance companies are no longer covering this loss, no matter the cause. Thus it is essential to (1) make certain that the causes of mold, that is, water and high humidity, are removed to prevent mold growth in the first place, and (2) that you review the amendments to your insurance policies and understand what is covered and what is not. If mold damage has been excluded from your policy, discuss this issue with your insurance agent, facilities management, and the disaster response team to forestall mold growth in the first place.

Contents

Insurance policies consider *contents* to be everything in a building or space that is not records, files, papers, and documents. The policy usually covers equipment, furniture, shelving, carpets, curtains, and everything else of this nature. As the institution or each department adds staff and uses more space, make certain the insurance policy keeps pace.

The insurance policy should cover the *replacement value* of the contents. In this way, the items could be replaced if irreparably damaged or dried and cleaned if they sustain minimal damage.

Valuable Papers

Every business, library, and information center should have a rider for valuable papers. This rider covers the damage or loss of documents, archives, books, art, paper records, journals, microfilm and microfiche, books, computer disks and CD-ROM, and so forth. In short, it covers all the items that make up a library. At some point in the past, an inventory with item values was taken, and insurance was based upon that replacement cost. If the inventory is outdated, the institution is underinsured for such a loss. It is important to look at the different caps in the insurance policy annually to make certain the library collection is adequately covered. Evaluate the policy at least every three years to adjust for inflation and the increase in size of the collection. The insurance policy should cover the replacement cost of about one-third of the collection. No insurance policy will be large enough to include funding for replacement of every title. It will limit the amount of money paid out.

If the library or archives contains a rare book room or special collections, you might consider a separate valuable papers rider for these items. Determine the average price for replaceable books in the rare book or special collections room. That should be the replacement cost, or "agreed amount" per volume. For a unique or valuable rare book collection, discuss how the valuable papers rider covers conservation costs, including drying, rebinding, and other conservation work.

An inventory of the titles may be requested to satisfy the insurance adjuster of the loss. Provide the titles or a count of the number of books and a range of costs for replacing the collection. Always include the cost of processing and cataloging materials in the replacement cost.

On the business side of the library, valuable papers include articles of incorporation, stocks and certificates, minutes, leases, and other legal papers that are essential to continue in business. To prevent loss, originals should be stored off-site in a safe-deposit box.

Computers

The computer rider covers the cost of replacing any item that involves computers and data. It usually covers renting space in a hot or cold site. Computer riders assume that you back up data appropriately and often and that you can get the data operational at the alternative site. The insurance policy usually will not cover reconstructing the lost data. The policy could cover the "recovery" of the physical objects, such as diskettes, tape and disk drives, and optical and laser discs.

Computer riders cover drying, cleaning, and reconditioning or recertifying the computer equipment. The more expensive the equipment, the more likely that the insurance company will insist on recovery and recertification of equipment.

This rider of the insurance policy will include "functional replacement." This is the correct type of replacement policy for computer equipment and peripherals, for it means that if you have older equipment, it may be possible to purchase newer equipment that performs the same functions and more.

Update the computer rider to include new equipment and configurations so the insurance policy adequately covers replacement.[2] Note the monetary and time limitations for recovering full computer operations in the insurance policy. Computer riders usually cover expenses and rental for two months.

Business Interruption or Extra Expense Insurance Rider

This rider covers renting equipment, space, furnishings, and phones; hiring temporary employees; and paying unemployment insurance, if needed. Business interruption or extra expense insurance should cover relocation and technology needs while in an alternative location. It includes covering payroll and accounts receivable/payable, up to a point. Business interruption insurance usually covers the reconstruction of paper documents and files *but not computer files*. There are many limits to business interruption insurance, including the duration of displacement and the amount of expenses that will be covered per month. The maximum duration is usually 12 months, but this varies depending upon the policy and projected needs.

Insurance Terminology

- Replacement cost—with like kind at current cost
- Actual cash value—the value of the item today. The amount is usually less than what it costs to replace an item or the fair market price.

- Functional replacement cost—with like kind to perform same functions
- Business interruption or extra expense insurance rider—pays costs to temporarily relocate, pays for lost income, has monetary limits and time constraints
- Average replacement cost—across-the-board average purchase price for each category of materials
- Coinsurance—(protects the insurance carrier) limits the reimbursement after a disaster. It is a cap on expenditures by the insurance company. Note that an insurance underwriter may cover some of the deductible and this policy has an upper limit where the major insurance carrier picks up coverage.

Contingency Funds

In addition to insurance, every library and information center should have a contingency fund to cover unexpected, uncovered expenses and the insurance deductible.

How much money is set aside to deal with a disaster depends upon available capital, projected risk, and the ability of the institution, library, archives, or historical society to raise funds in a short period of time. Money might be put aside to cover initial expenses until the insurance kicks in.

In the case of a national, state, or county-wide "declared disaster," the FEMA will probably require that you pay first and get reimbursed second. Try to submit the claim as a group, agency, government, or area. This will speed the reimbursement process.

Consider extra insurance riders when mounting valuable exhibits or sending materials for storage or treatment. A monetary value must be assigned to these items so that if they are damaged, the same or similar items could be purchased to replace them.

Replacement Costs

Work with your acquisitions and cataloging department to determine ahead of time replacement costs with processing. Approximate costs, including processing, follow:

- Books: replacing books costs $25 to $30 per volume of fiction; $50 to $150 for non-fiction; and $150 and up for reference tools.

- Audio books on cassette and CD/DVD: abridged $25 to $30 each, unabridged $50 to $150 each.

- Videos and DVD: $25 to $40 for popular fiction, $50 and up for non-fiction and educational series.

- Microfilm and microfiche: commercially produced film costs $100 to $150 per roll; independently produced microfilm is not expensive to duplicate ($10 to $25 per roll) if the master print positives or negatives are stored in a safe, off-site location.

- Software CD-ROMs: stand-alone products vary in price from $20 to $100 and up; products for LANs and networked systems depend upon site licensing fees.

- For special collections, rare books and archives, determining the replacement costs is a time-consuming task. You could have the collection appraised for total value. Then take a price to replace some of the replaceable items, say $300 to $400 each. Some books will cost less, some more to replace. But the sum total, if the entire collection were destroyed, will provide enough funds to begin building the collection again.

Modify these costs to match those of your institution.

Average costs to dry a book using dehumidification or vacuum freeze-drying are $5 to $10 per volume. Treatment is cost-effective even if the materials need to be bound afterward because of loss of structural integrity.[3] If you are having the dried volumes bound, discuss this with your binder and ask about special prices to keep the costs under control.

Communications

Communications is one of the aspects of disaster response that is often forgotten in the planning phase. There are three types of communications activities that should be planned:

1. with employees, and in a large institution, with other staff and departments;

2. with suppliers and customers, patrons, or clients; and

3. with the media and general public.

Before the crisis arises, discuss with the public information or communications officer how the library/archives will inform non-staff of the disaster. Decide who will handle the different aspects of communication. The ideal situation is to have the communications officer handle it all, or at least the outside communications, but part of the responsibility will undoubtedly fall upon the disaster response team leader or the director of the library, archives, or historical society.

Create a basic press release for the public and a script for informing staff of where to go and who will be needed when (see figure 4.2).

Send this information to the radio, TV, and newspapers, as well as suppliers, insurance carriers, the post office, and creditors. If the library/archives has a website, add the information there as well.

Communication with the Staff

Several decisions must be made, usually during the initial response phase, concerning staff communication. If it is a large disaster, are all the staff needed to deal with the disaster or just the disaster response team members? Do you want the staff there in shifts? Where should they report when they arrive at the "office" and to whom? The command center or external meeting location should be designated or identified ahead of time and how to get there. In the case of a small library or an information center within a corporation, is there a secondary location where some staff members should report? In the plan, list the phone number of the person to call who will tell staff where to report.

Employees of the institution should be notified how to contact the library or archives. Will the institution or certain departments be closed or immediately reopen at the secondary location? Where are they located? What are the temporary hours? What are the new phone and fax numbers and e-mail address? Where do staff go for information when the library is closed?

FIGURE 4.2. Sample Press Release for the Public and Media

The _____ Library is temporarily closed due to _____

_____ damage. Materials can be returned to the _____

_____ branch.

[or]

Please hold all materials from the library/archives. Fines will be suspended during the period the institu-

tion is closed.

[or]

The _____ Library is operating out of a temporary location

due to fire and water damage to the building. Our temporay location is _____

_____ .

The new phone number is _____ .

Our hours are _____ .

It is important to maintain good communications within the organization and keep the adminisration apprised of all unusual expenses, circumstances, and problems that arise. A liaison should be designated to communicate with the administration, preferably the director of the library or archives.

Communication with Suppliers and Customers

Maintaining contact with those who supply services, products, and equipment is crucial. They must know where to send products, how to communicate with you, and who is authorized to make emergency purchases and issue purchase orders.

For online and information services, new account numbers may be necessary. Supply temporary phone numbers and an address for billing and sending materials. Set up new passwords and security codes. Lease equipment, if necessary.

Customers need to be reassured that you will open and when. If there is a temporary location, let customers know where it is and what the hours are.

Communication with the Media and the General Public

It is important to have only one spokesperson for the institution. With the approval of the administration, this person should discuss what occurred. Indicate when the operation will be back up and running; what services are available; where the library, archives, or historical society is temporarily located; and what hours it is open.

Information about the disaster can and should be made available to the media. This will enable the institution to get publicity about the disaster, the collections, and services and to solicit assistance and donations.

It is important to remember that fund-raising and development campaigns, essential for non-profit and cultural institutions, are the most effective during the first six months after the disaster. If you need to rebuild the collection or the building, start the fund-raising and development campaign immediately.

When the Disaster Is Over

When the disaster is over, write articles and give interviews to let the institution, libraries, and archives, as well as the general community, know what happened during your crisis. If you wish donations of services and materials, specify what you want and in what format. For instance, if the library lost a large number of books and reference materials to a fire or flood, don't just ask for books. Request the titles or topics needed. Specify if you wish them to be cataloged and how.

If you are part of a consortium, enlist the organization's assistance with coordinating the acceptance of donations of services and materials. They can be a channel for communications and information. The consortium may have emergency response policies and services that your organization can take advantage of.

Most of all, don't be shy. Ask for help from friends, colleagues, and professionals in the area. The more people who know about the disaster, the more support you will receive, be it moral, emotional, physical, or financial.

Telecommunications

Just as communication with customers, suppliers, vendors, and staff is important, telecommunications is an integral part of the services provided by your institution. Without phones, fax machines, modems, and e-mail, outreach services and accessibility to information will deteriorate quickly. It is essential to be prepared for part or all of the telecommunications services to fail for some period of time.

- Determine how long telecommunications will be out before declaring a disaster and activating the plan.

- Make use of cellular, portable, and car phones. Set up a contingency contract with the local service.
- Contract with a second long-distance service so calls can continue to come in if the main system is down or overloaded.
- If local phone service is essential, consider a second, private company with its own phone lines.

Contacting Disaster Response Companies and Consultants

One of the aspects of disaster planning is to ask for assistance from knowledgeable consultants and outside contractors. Using the services of outsiders will relieve some of the stress from the disaster response team members. But you cannot just list contractors, consultants, and disaster response/drying companies in your plan; you should talk with them to find suitable contractors. Invite the ones you are interested in to visit the institution for a walk-through and discussion of their roles in potential disasters. In this way, they will become acquainted with the needs of your library/archives, know what they need to bring, and understand how to assist the disaster response team in responding to and recovering from the disaster.

Why use outsiders? After all, that is the job of the disaster response team, right? Well, if the disaster is small, then the disaster response team may be able to handle everything with the assistance of staff members and facilities maintenance. However, if the disaster area covers a large portion of the building or has created secondary damage, it is essential that outside contractors be called in to assist. Use their labor and expertise for advice and recommendations in the recovery and cleanup. Be certain to include the facilities maintenance department in these meetings so that (1) they will know what type of assistance is required during a disaster, and (2) they will be able to provide input in terms of selecting a contractor and assisting during the cleanup operation.

The following are some of the issues to discuss when you select and meet with outside contractors:

- What types of services they can actually provide for your institution
- How much of the work they do themselves and what types of work they contract out
- How much experience they have with libraries and archives disasters. Ask for references and check them out.
- How they ship, handle, and dry water-damaged materials
- What techniques they use to remove soot, dirt, and mold from items
- Costs for services and labor
- Emergency contact numbers for after-hours disasters
- Whether they have a "first come, first serve" policy or, if preapproved by the institution, you are the "first priority" during a wide-area disaster
- What types of information they keep on hand about institutions that have listed them in disaster response plans
- Whether they have specialists they can call in to treat unique and fragile items in the collection

Once you decide upon the contractor(s), write them into the response and recovery portions of the plan. Have an emergency purchase order issued or standing by, so that the initial amount of expenses is known and allocated. Preapproving the contractor as a vendor may save time. For insurance purposes and for dealing with the insurance adjuster, decide if you wish the vendor designated as a primary contractor(s).

Preselecting outside contractors decreases stress on staff, worry, and physical labor. It eliminates the need for the disaster response team to have to find suitable and qualified vendors *while* dealing with all the other issues and crises in the preliminary response phase.

Provide the contractor with a copy of your disaster response plan so he or she can be ready to perform the required services with less lead time. Having a copy of your plan will allow the contractor to make a list of necessary equipment and arrange for staff

and temporary help to get the job done quickly and correctly.

A side benefit of preapproving vendors is that stress on the facilities maintenance staff is decreased. The facilities maintenance staff should know how to contact the vendor, what services she or he is needed for, and what the contractor will provide. Assign a disaster response team or staff member as liaison to the contractor(s) and facilities maintenance department. This is particularly important if more than one building is involved in the disaster or if the disaster is widespread.

Two types of services can be contracted from the vendors of disaster response/drying services: cleanup and recovery.

Cleanup could be done by the facilities maintenance department itself or with the disaster response company as a subcontractor. These types of services fall under cleanup:

- Removing water
- Basic cleaning of the building, shelving, furnishings, etc.
- Removing debris, soot, dirt, and mold from surfaces

Recovery may be contracted out, especially if a large portion of the collection was damaged or if there is limited staff available. This is important if the library or archives has only a few staff members. These types of services fall under recovery:

- Drying and cleaning contents
- Drying and cleaning collections
- Removing dry and undamaged collections to an environmentally controlled facility if necessary
- Drying and cleaning (and recertifying) equipment, including office equipment and computers

During the planning and prevention phase, the leases and maintenance agreements for office and computer equipment should be reviewed. Determine the scope of "recovery" the maintenance contract includes, acceptable dealers or vendors to perform this work, and a list of where to lease or rent the needed equipment while damaged or wet equipment is being serviced.

Other services might be contracted out:

- Maintaining, cleaning, and calibrating the HVAC to balance the environment to where it was before the disaster
- Restoring computer services, including OPAC, LAN, and internal (non-public) computers
- Loading the backup databases, including the online catalog and such internal systems as payroll and financial information

Training

The primary purpose of training is to know what to do and how to channel energies and adrenaline when the disaster strikes. The secondary purpose is to have a basic idea of what actions need to be accomplished first.

There are two views on training. The first is to teach just the disaster response team, who will lead all the operations and will train the others on the fly when the disaster strikes. Each disaster response team member will have a specific group of responsibilities. The need to train on the spot will definitely occur when the disaster response team works with volunteers or temporary laborers brought in by the institution or the disaster response company to perform much of the manual labor necessary to move books, pack boxes, and clean surfaces.

The second training method is to make the entire staff aware of the plan and basic response actions and then provide additional training for the disaster response team and interested staff members. The second method, teaching the entire staff about the contents of the plan and the basics of disaster response, is preferred by preservation librarians and consultants but is not always accomplished before a disaster strikes. One of the best reasons to teach the staff about the disaster response plan and basic response methods is so that minor leaks, isolated water damage, mold, and other "small" emergencies can be handled locally by department members, especially if the disaster response team is not available. Teaching all the staff, or key members in each department, is very important if the library or archives is spread throughout a large building or is in many buildings.

Necessary Training

- Be aware of primary and secondary damage caused by water, especially mold and ozone.
- Understand the need to react; never assume that the next person will deal with the problem or that it is "not your job."
- Know who to call when the disaster occurs (disaster response team leader, administration, director); what to report (water, mold, fire, etc.); the extent of the damage; and who to call after regular working hours.
- Learn where the basic disaster response supplies are kept and how to use them.
- Discuss the decisions and rationale behind prioritization for recovery if the area or collection is damaged. Emphasize that changing the criteria during the response phase is not necessarily in the institution's best interest.

Additional Training

- Learn how to handle and move water-damaged materials.
- Learn methods of packing boxes for freezing and vacuum freeze-drying.
- Label boxes so materials are returned to the appropriate institution and department.
- Know how to deal with special collections and formats such as photographs, AV materials, and manuscripts. Discuss where the list is for specialists who can be called in to assist with their recovery.

Some hands-on disaster response training seminars involve teaching the use of fire extinguishers and fire hoses. This should be taught by professionals, either the fire department or a fire extinguisher or fire protection company. If your institution has a security department that handles small fires, ask them to provide a training session for the disaster response team members and other interested staff.

Fire extinguishers are not hard to use. Just set the canister upright on the floor, pull the pin or metal ring at the top of the handle, point the nozzle away from you, and squeeze the trigger handle. Make certain you do not touch the nozzle; the contents may be extremely cold and could freeze on contact! Fire extinguishers can be heavy to lift and operate. When in doubt, pull the fire alarm.

When should you use a fire extinguisher? On a small, self-contained fire only. Fire extinguishers have about 30 to 60 seconds worth of liquid. If the fire is larger than that or is spreading rapidly, walk quickly away from it and pull the fire alarm. Then leave the area and assemble staff in the designated location outside the building.

Disaster response team members should know where the fire extinguishers and hoses are, where the heat and smoke detectors ring, and what type of sprinkler system is in the building.

The more training, education, and awareness the staff and disaster response team members have, the more quickly and efficiently you will be able to respond to disasters and get them contained or at least organized for the recovery of the collection and services.

How and Where to Get Training in Disaster Response

- Read the multitude of books and articles available in libraries, archives, and computer and business literature.[4]
- Attend seminars sponsored by local and regional consortia and at conferences.

- Attend classes through the preservation departments in some universities or library science programs. Programs in continuing education in preservation are offered at Johns Hopkins, Pittsburgh University, University of Texas at Austin, Kent State University, and the University of Wisconsin at Madison.[5]
- Attend hands-on recovery classes that teach how to pack and handle water-damaged materials.
- Ask your consultants: consultants who work in disaster response often teach seminars on planning and response.

Some conservation centers sponsor specialized disaster response classes, especially about photographs, textiles, furniture, or works of art on canvas. If your institution has a large collection of any of these items, it would be worthwhile to either attend a seminar or have the name of specialized consultants who deal with these water-damaged items.

Follow up the planning and training phases by practicing the response plan. Evaluate the plan based on problems that arise in procedures when you practice, and revise accordingly. Don't forget to distribute the revisions to all the disaster response team members and insert the revisions in all the printed plans.

Establish a regular revision and evaluation schedule and stick to it. Keep the printed plans updated.

This final case study describes what happened to the main branch of the Metropolitan Library in Oklahoma City as a result of the bombing of the Murrah Federal Building on April 19, 1995.[6]

CASE STUDY FOUR

Firsthand Experience during the Oklahoma City Bombing

After the bombing of the Murrah Federal Building on April 19, 1995, the library director and staff stuck to their plan and followed all the response and recovery steps as outlined in their plan. The library staff were very fortunate that little of their collection was damaged; rather, it was access to the building and the area around it that was the problem, in addition to some minor physical damage to the interior. Lee Brawner, executive director, Metropolitan Library, Oklahoma City, Oklahoma, sent a copy of his firsthand experience with the disaster, which has been abridged.

Not unlike you, I had always assumed that disasters and catastrophes befell other libraries and not my own. Yes, my library did have an Emergency Operating Plan in place. We had conducted periodic evacuation drills in all the library buildings and had even taken our administrators through a couple of mock disasters. Our plan, while helpful, was not sufficient, and we were not fully prepared for the disaster that engulfed our city, our downtown library, and our staff in the spring of 1995.

The downtown library is constructed of reinforced concrete with about 110 windows on its three exposed elevations. Most of the windows face into offices, The library books and materials are located in the center of the floors; other materials are located in a windowless second-floor closed stack area.

On the morning of April 19, the downtown staff were in their offices or at public service desks. At 9:02, the circulation clerk was two minutes late approaching the heavy glass double doors with keys in hand to open the library to the public. I happened to be in the area. We looked away from the windows to answer a question, and in the next instant a shock wave hit, blowing us across the floor, through an open door, and down a short corridor. As we landed, a giant explosion deafened us, and we looked back to see the glass and frames of three windows blowing in and sending glass and debris into the office and across a table. We began hearing muffled, distant explosions and saw that windows had blown out in the adjoining offices and concluded it was not a plane crash, but we didn't know what it was. We heard screams and shouts for help from our third floor and found a staff member who had been hit in the head by flying glass. She had been sitting between the windows and an interior glass partition when both walls were blown out. We quickly discovered our first aid kits were too limited and practically useless to assist with injuries of this extent. We used clothing as compresses to stop the bleeding and began carrying the injured staff member out of the building. The rest of the staff were evacuating the building in an orderly fashion as we had rehearsed in many drills. It was fortunate the circulation staff member did not get the heavy glass front doors open before the explosion or they would have been blown in with great force. The glass transom above the front doors shattered and blew 20 feet into the building, and the glass side panels cracked but did not shatter.

Upon exiting the rear of the building into the alley toward our designated evacuation site, we were stunned by the scene. The air was filled with debris, paper, and dust swirling above and around the Murrah Federal Building a half block away, and we could hear muffled screams. A staff member froze and said quietly, "My god, this is the anniversary of the Waco Davidian fire!" We still had not comprehended what had happened. Facing the rear of the federal building, we could see daylight through the back and sides of its nine-story structure.

The scene was becoming more chaotic, and I made the decision to get all but a few staff out of the area. Three library maintenance staff were at the library. Even though we had made a head count on a department-by-department basis of all the staff, the maintenance staff swept the building looking for any other personnel. The maintenance staff briefly escorted staff back into the library to gather personal belongings and make phone calls. Although most of the ceiling lights on the fourth floor had been knocked out of their fixtures, we still had electricity. At this point, we realized that many of our emergency flashlights could not be easily located, and others did not work. After the building was cleared, we shut off the electricity, gas, and water.

When the staff reassembled, I asked all but the maintenance staff to go home and report the next morning to the Belle Isle Library (a large regional library in the system) for a briefing and work assignments. Going home proved difficult when we learned that many of the staff members' cars were damaged or blocked by damaged cars. Staff carpooled home.

In the meantime, I assigned several administrative staff members to begin setting up the meeting rooms at the Belle Isle Library and planning for telecommunications to accommodate extra staff and computer equipment. Three maintenance staff were asked to stay and secure the building.

Within one hour of the explosion, we had spoken with our insurance carrier, who advised us to take all the necessary actions to care for the staff and secure the building and contents. He said an adjuster would be there the next day. The maintenance supervisor obtained plywood and other materials to secure the building. The plywood in the area ran out quickly. Later that evening I went, along with eight maintenance staff and two volunteer carpenters, to temporarily secure the windows with plywood and, when that ran out, with plastic.

The next morning, the downtown staff met at the Belle Isle Library. They were briefed on the status of the two injured staff members and the condition of the building. We had already started implementing our response plan by caring for staff injuries and shock and protecting the building, furnishings, and materials. I had arranged for one of the community's leading psychologists and counselors on post-traumatic stress syndrome to present an information session. He emphasized that everyone in the community—co-workers who were not in the downtown library, family, neighbors, and others—had been impacted by the disaster. He described the effects of post-traumatic stress syndrome and how to respond to its symptoms. The administration urged staff to seek individual counseling if needed.

A few of the staff were dispatched with the library's security officer to see if they could gain access to the tightly secured area to retrieve key administrative documents, business and personnel files, and funds and documents from administration's safe. We confirmed that the library's computerized records were not damaged, as the mainframe is not housed in the downtown library.

From the first day after the bombing until the move back into the downtown library, the library's public information officer issued daily reports to all other library agencies on the status of the library staff, the interim operations, and related news. The office also sent communications to the state library, which subsequently distributed the information across the state. The public information officer sent news releases to the national library media and responded to a wide range of local and national media inquiries.

We continued to implement our response and recovery plan by doing the following:

- Assigning staff to alternate work locations
- Engaging a counselor to help staff deal with post-traumatic stress
- Retrieving key files, documents, and monies so we could operate off-site
- Assigning staff duties for the interim operating period
- Obtaining furnishings, computers, and communications at the temporary work sites
- Revising work schedules to ease staff stress. All downtown library staff worked five six-hour days until the building reopened.
- Establishing communications with staff in the rest of the system and the libraries in the state
- Contracting a structural engineer to check for damage to the building
- Arranging with a disaster response company to clean the building and equipment
- Repairing the windows, light fixtures, walls, etc.

On the third day after the bombing, the administration contracted with a local structural engineer to assess the downtown library in terms of structural damage and needed repairs. Primarily, the windows and light fixtures needed replacing. In addition, we contacted a disaster response company to clean up the glass and debris, remove the dust and dirt from all surfaces, and vacuum the carpeted areas and furnishings, as well as all the electronic and computer equipment.

After the building was cleaned and repaired, the staff returned to the building to clean the books and shelves. The building reopened within 35 days of the bombing.

Some facts and figures: The library received more than 700 communications from libraries and the public, offering help and encouragement. More than $30,000 in unsolicited funds and books were donated, mostly for the children's room. The total cost to clean and repair was $115,000. We were fortunate that the library collection was spared.

The closing comment to Lee Brawner's presentation follows:

One of my heroes, the late Joseph Campbell, scholar and philosopher, observed "It is by going down into the abyss that we recover the treasures of life." And he wrote, "Opportunities to find deeper powers within ourselves come when life seems most challenging."

The events in our city and our library in the wake of the bombing changed and challenged us, and we now strive to reflect on the treasures and not the tragedies of April 19, 1995.

Endnotes

1. Reagan Moore, et al., *Collection-Based Persistent Archives,* available at http://www.sdsc.edu/NARA/Publications/OTHER/Persistent/Persistent.html; also Gregory Hunter, *Preserving Digital Information* (New York: Neal-Schuman, 2000).

2. Use the checklists for hardware and software in appendix A to keep track of what each department has.

3. George Cunha, "Disaster Planning and a Guide to Recovery Resources," *Library Technology Reports* (September/October 1992): 542f.

4. See the bibliography at the end of this book.

5. CoOL (Conservation OnLine) contains information about seminars, conferences, and classes in preservation and is available at http://palimpsest.stanford.edu/. Information for subscribing to the Conservation Discussion List (ConsDist.Lst) and links to other preservation and conservation sites are available at CoOL.

6. Text was provided by Lee Brawner, executive director, Metropolitan Library, Oklahoma City, with permission to edit and publish.

Response and Recovery Procedures

Basic Response Procedures

Fire

- Call fire and police departments.
- Evacuate the building.
- Meet at the prearranged location.
- Activate the disaster response plan.
- Notify the insurance company.

Flood/Water

- Get the water turned off.
- Activate the disaster response plan.
- Notify the insurance company.
- Call a disaster response/drying company to have the water removed.

Power Outage

- Initiate controlled shutdown of the computer system.
- Notify the power company of the power outage.
- Initiate paper-based procedures.

- Assemble the disaster response team and decide whether to relocate online services while the power is out.
- Send a press release to the media with information about temporary location, hours, and emergency phone numbers.

Telecommunications Outage

- Locate or rent cellular phones.
- Notify the phone company of the outage.
- Send a press release to the media with information about temporary location, hours, and emergency phone numbers.

Computer Crash

- Contact the computer systems operator or information systems librarian.
- Identify the cause of failure.
- Notify the insurance company.
- Arrange to replace damaged equipment.
- Reload software and data.

Computer Theft/Damage

- Contact the computer systems operator or information systems specialist.
- Contact the insurance company.
- Locate hardware and software checklists.
- Contact a computer rental company to deliver necessary equipment.
- Load software and data.

Building or Institution Inaccessible

- Notify staff of alternative location.
- Arrange for phone service.
- Contact a computer rental company to deliver necessary hardware and software.
- Send a press release to the media with information about temporary location, hours, and emergency phone numbers.

Packing Procedures for Books, Documents, Archives, and Office Files

Removing Water-Damaged Books, Documents, Archives, and Office Files

- Remove items lying on the floor first.
- Remove items from shelves in order, starting at the top shelf.
- Move materials to a packing area, and try to maintain the order of the items.
- Pack items in ordinary boxes, setting them flat on the bottom, or in document file boxes. Do not jam materials into the boxes.
- Count the number of items in the box as you work.
- Label each box with the number of items, format or type, location, and box number (for example: 27 Books, Science Library, OSU, Box 36; or 125 Microfilms, Government Documents, U Mich., Box 105).
- List each box on the inventory sheet.
- Seal the boxes with tape and move them to a loading area.

- Send one copy of the inventory with the boxes; keep one copy for the disaster response team and one for the insurance company.

Wet Document Storage Boxes

- Remove files.
- Place dry materials only in new dry boxes.
- Pack wet materials vertically in boxes or milk crates.
- Label the boxes with contents information before shipping.

Loose Documents or Manuscripts in Filing Cabinets

If contents are filed vertically,

- remove contents from drawers;
- if materials are soaked or in colored folders, wrap them in precut freezer paper, shiny side toward documents;
- place contents vertically in boxes or milk crates for transport;
- label the boxes with contents information before shipping;
- list each box on the inventory sheet; and
- seal the boxes with tape and move them to a loading area.

Note: If filing cabinet drawers are stuck shut from the force of wet files and papers, use a crowbar to open them.

If contents are stored in flat file drawers,

- use Mylar to remove (see the directions for handling large format materials later in this section);
- place wet documents on the shiny side of precut freezer paper;
- pack documents flat in bread trays or on cardboard. Tape Mylar or cardboard on top of trays to prevent damage or loss;
- label the trays with contents information before shipping;
- list each tray on the inventory sheet; and
- move them to a loading area.

Note: Materials will not look "pristine" when returned. They may be wrinkled and distorted if they were wrinkled before being frozen.

Selecting a Drying Method— Dehumidification vs. Vacuum Freeze-Drying

Each drying job is slightly different. The following four factors must be considered before selecting a drying method.

1. How long the items have been wet
2. How many items are wet
3. If they have monetary or legal value
4. Where you want the materials dried

Factors and First Decisions

How Long the Materials Have Been Wet and What Type They Are

If paper is wet for several days and begins to dry without any control, it can form a block of cellulose or the pages may stick together. Clay-coated, or shiny, paper is notorious for sticking together solidly within hours of getting wet. Plain paper can handle a few days of being submerged in water. Soaked paper that dries on its own can either dry in sheets and come apart, or it will form a solid block of cellulose and be useless.

If paper is *slightly* wet or the moisture content is just above 8 percent and there is not a lot of paper (less than 10 cubic feet), then dehumidification is the easiest method for drying.

If paper is soaked, vacuum freeze-drying is most appropriate.

For clay-coated paper, vacuum freeze-drying is the best method to use, provided the paper is stabilized and frozen within six hours of exposure to water. There is only a 50 percent success rate in drying clay-coated paper, no matter what drying method is used.

Estimate the Number of Items That Are Wet

If there are only several cartons or cubic feet of wet items, the method may not matter as much as if there are roomfuls or thousands of cubic feet to dry. Most paper, whether bound into books and journals or loose, can be frozen. Do not freeze leather- or vellum-bound materials without consulting the preservation officer or a conservator.

Consider the following rules of thumb.

- If there are more than 10 cubic feet or document storage cartons, contract out the drying.
- If there are more than 500 volumes, contract out the drying.
- If there are less than these quantities and you have the space, dehumidify the room and provide air movement. *Remember,* wet paper may wrinkle or cockle, and distort bindings, if air dried.

When in doubt, freeze items as quickly as possible. This accomplishes two things: it buys time to make decisions and raise money and permits treatment in manageable batches. Freezing will forestall a mold infection in the books and building. Unless the collection is contaminated with a hazardous waste, the frozen items do not pose a health threat. Ask the freezer/cold storage company to cold shrink-wrap the cartons onto skids, after labeling for easy identification. (Cold shrink-wrap is plastic that sticks together without heat. Skids are wooden pallets.)

Freezing quickly provides another benefit. The ice crystals that form are smaller and less likely to harm or deform the surface of items. The slower the freezing, the larger the ice crystals and the greater the chance for damage.

Items with Monetary or Legal Value: For collections with monetary value, contact a conservator or conservation center and ask how the materials should be shipped to them.[1] Some conservation centers want the materials shipped wet if they can be treated immediately; other items may be frozen to permit time to treat. Inquire about leather and vellum before freezing these items.

Collections with legal value are often the permanent records of the organization or institution and may include the articles of incorporation (see checklist number 17 in appendix A). If these items are the originals, they will need to be dried and cleaned. However, the original versions of permanent, vital, and legal records should be stored off-site, with copies and microfilm on-site. If the duplicates were damaged, they should be destroyed and discarded.

Where You Want Materials Dried: If you must keep items on-site (for security reasons, etc.), then dehumidification and air drying are your only options. If materials can be removed from the building, then dehumidification and vacuum freeze-drying are your drying options. Note that the vacuum freeze-drying process is the only process that does not require removing items from their boxes. Dehumidification and air drying require removal of items from boxes to make certain all surfaces are dry.

Vacuum freeze-drying and dehumidification off-site take at least three or four weeks, depending upon how wet the materials are and how soon the disaster response/drying company can get the materials into the drying chambers.

The only manner of drying available for collections that must remain on-site is dehumidification, or air drying by spreading out books and papers onto flat surfaces, while providing air movement with fans to make the paper dry. Air drying in-house (with fans) with the institution's staff is very labor-intensive, requires security, and has the potential side effects of distortion of paper and swollen bindings.

Preliminary Treatment

Clay-Coated Paper: Interleave clay-coated, or shiny, paper with precut freezer paper or double-sided wax paper, shiny side toward text, if labor and time permit. Soaked clay-coated paper will stick together permanently within six hours. Clay-coated paper can be stored in water for a short while until there is time to treat it. Be aware that the printing is often imbedded in the clay and can dissolve and wash away from the surface of the paper. If there is not sufficient time to interleave clay-coated paper, then freeze it and vacuum freeze-dry. Vacuum freeze-drying provides better end results than dehumidification or air drying. The success rate is about 50 percent regardless of the drying method used. Many libraries and archives choose to discard clay-coated materials if they are easily replaceable or duplicated on microfilm. Decide during the prioritization phase if you will keep water-damaged clay-coated paper.

Only treat or discard clay-coated paper if it is damaged. Otherwise, store it in a dry location.

Photographs, Negatives, and Film: Separate photographic materials into different processes, if possible, and remove from paper envelopes before drying. Do not let photographic materials dry by themselves in boxes, folders, or sleeves. Quickly freeze photographs if unable to treat them immediately *and if this method is approved by the preservation or conservation officer.* There is a chance that freezing will damage the surface of photographs. Ask a conservator before freezing photographic materials with monetary or artistic value.

Magnetic Tape: Remove magnetic tape from the water as soon as possible. *Do not freeze it.* If the magnetic tape is unique or the backup tape has been destroyed, send it to be dried, cleaned, and copied onto a new tape. Some of the disaster response/drying companies can provide this service for you. If the magnetic tape is not unique *and* has been water damaged, discard and replace it.

When Paper Dries

Paper changes in character and form as soon as it gets wet. Paper also changes shape when exposed to high humidity or when it is stored under extremely dry conditions. Wrinkling or cockling is an indication that moisture was present and the paper dried slowly.

What causes this? Paper fibers expand when exposed to water or humidity. When the paper dries, the fibers shrink but at different rates. The more control of the paper's shape during the drying process, the less visible the cockling when the fibers shrink back to "normal."

Wetting and then drying cellulose or paper fibers has an adverse effect on the strength and mechanical properties of paper. Drying paper without restraint or control will result in cockling.

Choice of drying method can influence the amount of distortion. How much paper becomes distorted depends upon how wet the papers were when they were removed from the water or area of high humidity. Paper dries from the outside in, that is, from the fore edge to the binding. If dehumidification is the drying method used, carefully monitor the condition of the paper and the moisture content of the paper at the spine of the book or the center of the folder. Watch for deterioration of paper and mold growth.

Vacuum freeze-drying can reduce the amount of cockling, but there is no guarantee how materials will look when they are dry. If materials go into a dehumidifying or vacuum freeze-drying chamber wrinkled, they will come out that way. Dehumidification and vacuum thermal-drying, in and of themselves, can cause wrinkling or cockling because the items stay wet until all the excess moisture is removed. Those methods are okay for damp and slightly wet materials. Vacuum freeze-drying does not permit the item to get wet again, reducing the chance of wrinkling. Paper looks no worse than when it went into the drying chamber. This process is most suitable for soaked and clay-coated materials.

Drying Processes

In all drying processes, the moisture content of paper is usually *too low* after the drying treatment is completed. Use a meter to read moisture level. The moisture content must be increased to 6 percent to 8 percent. Paper will stabilize to the moisture content of the surrounding air on its own. Adjust the temperature and relative humidity slowly until it is the same as in the location the materials are shelved to prevent mold outbreaks.

Keep in mind these other factors when selecting a drying method:

- If the items are needed on-site or close by, then dehumidification may be the only choice. Vacuum freeze- and thermal-drying chambers are not usually mobile.

- Soaked materials and clay-coated paper should be vacuum freeze-dried.

- Photographs, film-based materials, and leather and vellum may be dehumidified or vacuum freeze-dried if acceptable to your conservator.

- Vacuum freeze-drying chambers are safe and secure because materials are dried in the boxes they were shipped in. Contents may be removed when dried using dehumidification.

- Prices for all types of drying treatments are similar, ranging from $45 to $65 per cubic foot (10 to 25 books) or $5 to $10 per book. Labor

for packing and cleaning and shipping charges are extra.

Desiccant Dehumidification: A desiccant dehumidifier traps and absorbs moisture in the air while still in a gaseous state as it moves across the desiccant's surface. Dry air is pumped out the other side of the machine. Desiccant dehumidifiers can dry the air to less than 30 percent rH. With careful monitoring, the environment can be controlled precisely. The equipment doesn't need to be physically in the building; ducts can pump moist air out of the building while fans move the air around. Desiccant dehumidification will make the air very hot. Require that the drying company maintain temperatures below 72° Fahrenheit. Higher temperatures can damage paper- and film-based materials. Desiccant dehumidification works well at cold temperatures and is efficient in large or small spaces, depending upon the size of the equipment. This method is excellent for drying photographs, film, negatives, X-rays, and microfilm/microfiche. Remember, however, adhesives may release from covers and spines of bound materials after prolonged exposure to moisture requiring rebinding of books. Desiccant dehumidification is great for drying out buildings after water damage has occurred.

Refrigerant Dehumidification: This technique condenses moisture from the air onto coils and then into a drip pan. Then the water must be flushed into a drainage system or emptied regularly. If the water is not removed from the refrigerant dehumidifier, the air will rehumidify, especially if the air is warm. The process of condensing moisture onto coils makes refrigerant dehumidification less effective at cooler temperatures. Refrigerant dehumidification can dry the air to 30 percent rH. This drying method also warms the air but not as much as desiccant. Refrigerant dehumidification equipment is portable and available in small units that condense and collect water within the unit. It is excellent for small drying jobs.

Vacuum Thermal-Drying: With vacuum thermal-drying, materials often enter the chamber in a frozen state. A vacuum is introduced, and the air is heated to between 50° and 100° Fahrenheit. The ice thaws and melts; *then* the water is turned into a gas, which is pumped out of the chambers. Contents become wet again and may cockle or wrinkle the paper during the drying process. The vacuum thermal-drying process may produce extreme warping of cellulose fibers due to the release of adhesives in bindings and under cloth covers when they are exposed to heat or prolonged moisture. Rebinding of books may be required.

Note: Water-soluble inks may run. Coated papers may stick together as a result of heat and the reintroduction of water. Vacuum thermal-drying is not suitable for leather or vellum materials.

Vacuum Freeze-Drying: With vacuum freeze-drying, items can go into the chamber frozen or wet. First, a vacuum is introduced, but *no heat is added.* Contents are dried at 32° Fahrenheit or colder in the vacuum chamber. As the vacuum is reduced, *ice is sublimated into vapor*—that is, the ice is changed directly into a gas and pumped out of the chamber immediately. Therefore, materials stay frozen until they dry. This is the best method for drying clay-coated papers if they were frozen within six hours of exposure to water. Vacuum freeze-drying may be suitable for water-soluble inks; check with a paper conservator first. When vacuum freeze-drying is used, less rebinding of previously wet materials is required. Check with a conservator before vacuum freeze-drying leather, vellum, or pre-1950 photographic processes.

Air Drying: This process involves using the institution's air-handling, or HVAC, system in conjunction with fans and portable dehumidifiers. This method can be used in very small areas and with small collections that are water damaged. Air drying presents the greatest chance for paper distortion, structural damage to paper and bindings, and mold growth.

Air drying is perceived to be the least expensive drying method for libraries and archives, but it is extremely time- and labor-intensive for the staff involved.

Film, photographs, negatives, X-rays, microfilm, and microfiche can all be air dried quickly, using dehumidification and air movement from fans. Just hang the items up on a clothesline made of plastic fishing wire or monofilament with plastic clips. Environmental conditions should be 65° to 70° Fahrenheit with a maximum of 55 percent rH and active air movement.

After materials have dried, remove soot, dirt, and mold. Removing such particulate matter before paper or photographs are dry may create permanent staining and will be nearly impossible to accomplish.

Documents and Files In-house— Handling and Drying Methods

Goal: Dry materials with dehumidifiers in-house so their moisture content is 6 percent to 8 percent. Then slowly adjust the relative humidity in the drying room to that of the area where they will be returned. This is done to prevent a mold infection.

The wet area must be dried completely. Relative humidity and temperature must be stabilized. Environmental conditions should be 45 percent to 55 percent relative humidity and 65° to 72° Fahrenheit. When the environment in the building is stabilized, adjust the drying room to the same environment. Watch for mold. When the moisture content of the paper is 6 percent to 8 percent in the drying room, you can move the materials back.

Drying Room

- Isolate an area so that humidity and air movement can be controlled.

- Segregate dry materials from wet. Store dry materials in a controlled environment away from high humidity.

- Set relative humidity as low as possible (35 percent to 45 percent) but no higher than 55 percent. Temperature should be as low as possible (65° to 72° Fahrenheit). Keep temperature and relative humidity stable. There should be no dead air pockets in the room.

- Set up shelves, racks, or tables for the files and books.

Procedures

- Remove files, documents, and bound materials from one box at a time. Try to maintain the shelf or filing order.

- Put files into milk crates, standing up. Do not jam documents into crates. Provide support to prevent sagging and distortion. Put books on tables upside down or on their spines while providing support. Bound materials should be rotated every six to eight hours to prevent irreparable damage to binding structure.
- Separate self-carboned and thermal-fax paper; they become sticky when wet.
- Decrease temperature and relative humidity and increase air movement, preventing mold growth. *Do not blow air on items directly.*
- When the moisture content of paper is 6 percent to 8 percent, paper is dry.
- Replace materials in the proper folders and label folders with contents.
- Return items to the shelves.

Books and Paper Files In-house— Handling and Drying Methods

Temperature

- As cold as possible
- No temperatures above 72° Fahrenheit

Note: High temperatures will decrease the life of paper and photographic materials, causing irreparable aging and such secondary damage as release of adhesives and distortion of bindings.

Humidity

- As low as possible
- Moisture content of paper should read 6 percent to 8 percent when dry

Note: Very dry air can cause paper and film to become brittle.

For very hygroscopic materials (such as leather, vellum, textiles, furniture, and framed works of art on canvas),

- very slowly reduce humidity to prevent additional distortion and to prevent structural damage; and
- contact conservators who specialize in these formats before treating or stabilizing.

Before accepting dried materials back from the disaster response/drying company,

- stabilize temperatures in the institution to prevent absorption of excess moisture and to prevent a mold infection; and
- clean the area and get it ready for shelving materials.

Large Format Materials— Handling and Drying Methods

Large format, or oversize, materials are difficult to handle when wet. Large format materials include, but are not limited to, maps, posters, broadsides, blueprints and architectural drawings, and works of art on paper. These materials are usually larger than 11-by-17 inches. They are printed on a variety of materials, including paper, Mylar, cloth, and coated stock. The combination of size and material creates difficulties carrying, separating, and physically handling them. Drying jobs that involve these materials must be performed by at least two people working together.

Large format materials can be found in map rooms, government document depositories, and science departments. Archives and historical societies that contain historical records and blueprints; art, art history, and popular cultural collections; and records centers often house large format materials. Some rare book and special collections may contain large format materials. Of course, large format materials are stored in architectural and engineering departments and building maintenance offices.

These materials can be stored in a variety of ways:

- Flat in drawers or cabinets
- Rolled, stored on end, or on their sides
- Rolled on a pole and stored vertically or horizontally
- Folded in filing cabinets
- Hung in vertical cabinets

Large format materials may be in poor condition because of the type of paper or cloth, the age of the item, or excessive handling by the public and staff.

If there is a lack of storage space in the institution, large format materials may be relegated to basements, storage closets, or attics. These collections should have been identified during the prioritization phase and ranked for recovery.

Removing Large Format Materials from the Building or Water-Damaged Area

Wet large format materials should be handled by teams of two.

- Remove water from any drawers or cabinets before moving the materials.
- Place a sheet of Mylar, Remay (a polyester spun cloth), or plastic over the top of materials before moving them. Covering these materials protects them from dirt and soot as well as prevents loss of items and accidental damage during transport.
- If necessary, move and freeze items in the drawers. Cover the drawer with Remay or Mylar to prevent loss or damage.
- Covered material may remain in place in the vacuum freeze-drying chamber.
- If air drying, remove items from the drawers (use procedures listed below) and dry flat under white blotter paper and weights.
- Check with a conservator before handling or drying works of art on paper.

Removing Large Format Materials from Drawers

All these procedures require at least two people working together.

File Folders in Drawers

- Remove by folder first. The folder may be so wet it requires additional support.
- Slip a sheet of Mylar larger than the folder under the folder and lift up.
- Place it flat on a table or a bread tray or any large, flat movable surface. Be careful not to tear wet items.
- Transport items to a vacuum freeze-drying chamber or a freezer to await drying.

Loose in Drawers

- Slip a sheet of Mylar larger than the materials into the drawer and under the materials.
- Lift up and place items flat on a table or bread tray.
- Transport items to a vacuum freeze-drying chamber or a freezer to await drying.

Separating Wet Large Format Materials

To separate wet large format materials, use sheets of Mylar that are larger than the materials. Mylar is better than plastic sheeting because it provides additional support. If Mylar is unavailable, plastic sheeting or Remay can be used. Mylar items, such as maps and architectural blueprints, should be hung to dry, not separated with Mylar, plastic sheeting, or Remay.

Paper Items

- Place the Mylar on top of the item and lift up slowly. The static electricity in the Mylar makes the paper stick to it and allows you to lift it up. Do not attempt to separate paper using your hands. The paper will tear.
- Place the item flat on blotter paper or Remay.
- Items should be dried face up.

Note: Some large format materials, such as art and posters, may have water-soluble inks, which will run when wet. Do not touch these materials with your hands. Place them face up on blotter paper or Remay. Contact a conservator to treat.

Mylar Items

- Mylar should separate if pulled apart slowly. Be careful, because Mylar can rip.
- Dry items flat or hang on monofilament with plastic clothespins.
- Do not allow Mylar to dry together; it may fuse permanently.

Linen or Cloth Items

- Use Mylar to separate.
- Cloth becomes very heavy and fragile when wet.

- The older the materials, the more fragile. Many colors will run when wet.
- Dry face up on white blotter paper or Remay. Contact a conservator to treat.

Encapsulated Items

- Open each item along the seam or tape.
- Place the item face down.
- Remove the Mylar carefully; turn the item over onto blotter paper, so it is face up; and remove the other sheet of Mylar.

Supplies for Drying Large Format Materials

- White blotter paper or Remay
- Mylar sheets (40-by-60 inches) or plastic cut to size
- Monofilament
- Plastic clothespins
- Bread trays or flat drying racks that support each item
- Lots of flat surfaces for drying

Potential Problems

Large format materials, when wet, may be problems to dry. The following types of problems may exist.

Maps 11-by-17 Inches or Larger

- Maps are fragile when wet.
- They will shred if not supported.
- Use Mylar or Remay to lift and move or separate wet sheets.
- Dry maps flat under blotters or weights. Watch for colored inks—they may bleed when wet.
- If the maps are encapsulated in Mylar, remove the top sheet of encapsulation and dry; then, encapsulate between new sheets of Mylar with new buffered sheets of paper or card stock for support.
- Contact a conservator if there is a large quantity of wet maps.

Posters

- Posters are often backed or mounted.
- If the posters are encapsulated in Mylar, remove the top sheet of encapsulation and dry.
- Encapsulate between new sheets of Mylar with new buffered sheets of paper or card stock for support.
- If the posters are colored, contact a conservator for advice about drying processes.

Blueprints, Architectural Drawings, and Engineering Prints

- Blueprints, usually printed on paper that is acidic by nature, are created using a diazo process.
- They become brittle with age.
- Blueprints are usually rolled and wrinkled.
- Poor storage conditions are not unusual.
- They shred when wet and are extremely fragile, so handle with care.
- Dry flat on white blotter paper or Remay.
- Treat only if there are no "exact" copies *and* they have monetary or artifactual value.

Linen Tracings

- Linen tracings become sticky when wet.
- They may separate, if you are lucky.
- They lose their finish when exposed to water.
- Dry flat on white blotter paper or Remay.

Mylar Tracings

- Mylar tracings will stick together on contact when wet.
- They will stay wet for months if untreated.
- If left wet and under pressure for long enough, approximately six months, Mylar tracings will stick together permanently.
- Separating stuck sheets may lift off printing.
- Dry flat or hang on monofilament with plastic clothespins.
- Do *not* fold. They will "learn" this position permanently.

If blueprints, architectural drawings, and engineering prints are available on microfilm, microfiche, or aperture card, then only small reproductions of originals remain, which microfilm reader/printers cannot enlarge to scale or original size. If patrons need to use blueprints, architectural drawings, or engineering prints in their original size, make the extra effort to treat the large format items.

Modern Film-Based Materials 1950–Present—Handling and Drying Methods

Film-based materials from 1950 to the present include

- photographic prints,
- motion picture film,
- microfilm and microfiche, and
- slides and negatives.

This information applies to film-based and photographic prints that were created after 1950. Items older than 1950 may be constructed of different elements and require very special handling and treatment, as the elements are unstable and extremely susceptible to moisture and exposure to water. Some will deteriorate or separate upon exposure to water. If you have a large photography collection that contains pre-1950 processes, contact a photograph conservator about procedures for stabilization and treatment if they are water damaged. These items should be identified during the prioritization phase and ranked for recovery. Detailed information for dealing with water damaged pre-1950s photographs can be found in *Care and Identification of 19th-Century Photographic Prints* by James M. Reilly and in *Disaster Recovery: Salvaging Photograph Collections* by Debra Hess Norris.

Photographs of all ages should be stored properly in sleeves of Mylar or paper and in appropriate storage containers such as file cabinets and boxes. Early photographs and those susceptible to water should not be stored near or under water pipes. All photographs and film should be stored at least a foot off the floor.

Photographic prints that were developed and processed after 1950 are constructed out of paper and an emulsion surface, which contains the photograph. Prints are able to withstand water for several days. However, as the surface of the film starts to dry, it will stick to whatever is touching it. Therefore, photographs should be kept wet until you are able to treat them and then hang up to dry on monofilament with plastic clothespins. If you are unable to treat the photographs within three days of getting wet *and* they do not have monetary value, freeze them (they can be vacuum freeze-dried at a later time). The photographs curl while drying. A conservator or professional photographer can assist you in flattening the prints once they are dry.

Modern motion picture film has an acetate base or a polyester base with emulsion. Pre-1950 film could have a nitrate base or an acetate base. Acetate is sometimes called "safety film." This is usually printed along the edge of the film.

Nitrate film is flammable if it has deteriorated. It is fairly stable if intact and stored appropriately. Motion picture and photograph archives that have nitrate film should store it in a separate location, below 32° Fahrenheit, with lots of air circulation. Mark on the floor plans where it is located. If undamaged in the disaster and in a safe, stable environment, leave it alone. If damaged during the disaster, contact the fire department for appropriate disposal, for it is categorized as a hazardous material. Consult a conservator before discarding the nitrate film to determine if it can be copied or salvaged.

Microfilm comes in a variety of types: silver halide, diazo, or vesicular. Master negatives and positives are usually made on silver halide. Master positives and negatives should be stored off-site at a depository such as Iron Mountain, Pennsylvania. Masters are the most valuable version because they are the original copies of microfilm, especially if they were created during "brittle books" programs, where the original hard-copy books were destroyed after filming. If masters are stored on-site, identify these during the prioritization phase and rank for recovery.

Microfilm or microfiche for everyday use is made on diazo or vesicular film. Both are fairly stable and can handle some exposure to water, although 72 hours is the maximum recommended without professional reprocessing. If the master negative or positive is intact, discard the use copy and make a new one. If not, then reprocess the use copy.

Slides are merely pieces of film that have been cut into individual frames and mounted in cardboard or plastic. If the slide collection is housed in plastic sleeves or sheets *and* it is wet, remove the slides from their housing as quickly as possible or immerse in water (for up to three days). Hang the slides to dry. Flatten and mount after they are dry. If you do not have time to do this *and* the collection does not have monetary value, freeze the pages. If the slides were frozen, discuss the side effects of thawing or vacuum freeze-drying with a photograph conservator. These suggestions for stabilization and treatment are suitable for negatives processed after 1950. Consult a photograph conservator for pre-1950 processes.

Deterioration of Film

All film is constructed in a similar manner of three layers: the base, the binder, and the emulsion. Other terms for these layers are *support, interlayer,* and *image-bearing layer,* respectively.

The base can be made of polyester, acetate, or nitrate. Polyester and acetate are the two most common types.

The emulsion, or image-bearing layer, usually has microscopic particles of silver that are chemically changed during exposure to light, processing, and, later, storage and atmospheric pollutants. High humidity can also damage the image, or emulsion layer. The silver particles are what create the image on the film.

The binder, or interlayer, is a very thin layer of adhesive called *gelatin* that attaches the emulsion to the base. When the binder deteriorates, the emulsion will flake or slide off the base. The binder is susceptible to moisture and environmental changes. If slightly moist, the emulsion will stick to whatever it touches.

Color film is composed of the same layers. The image-bearing layer contains the dyes. These are very susceptible to damage due to light and storage and environmental conditions. The color fades and changes as the film ages.

Reactions of Film to Water

Some modern films react slowly to water; others begin decomposition immediately. After 72 hours there is a greater risk of the emulsion flaking or sliding off. It is essential that you keep the photographs wet until you are ready to handle them. If allowed to dry on their own, the emulsion of the photograph or film will stick to whatever it is touching. Once this happens, it is almost impossible to separate them. Freeze the film if you are unable to stabilize it within 72 hours. Do not freeze photographs without discussing this with a photograph conservator. It is best to remove all film from sleeves, folders, and binders, as the emulsion will stick to the paper or Mylar. You will need to keep track of which photograph or slide goes with which sleeve, otherwise the provenance and description of the item are lost. Mold can form under the emulsion, eating away at the gelatin and destroying the images.

Soot, smoke, and pollution are all types of particulate matter—small particles that become trapped under and in emulsion. Particulate matter and pollution are not always removable and may stain, oxidize, and scratch the image on the film.

Stabilizing and Drying Film-Based Materials

Before drying or treating film-based materials, remove all items from paper or Mylar sleeves and folders to prevent sticking of emulsion to surfaces. This should be done before the items dry. If the negatives, film, or photographs are stuck together, there are no guarantees that soaking them in water will cause the base and emulsion to separate. Do not pull or force apart. It is important to maintain the order of the film, sleeves, containers, etc. Many items do not have contents indicated on film.

If you have older photographs and film-based materials in your collection, it is a good idea to talk with a photograph conservator before treating water-damaged photographs. A preliminary consultation should take place while surveying the collection during the planning phase of your disaster response plan.

Drying Options

- Vacuum freeze-dry film-based materials only if they have no monetary or artifactual value, as treatment may leave non-glossy patches on surface. Do not use the vacuum thermal drying process as it will cause the photograph to flake and distort.
- Dehumidification and air drying are also suitable treatments. Do not worry if photographs or negatives curl when drying. A conservator can help you flatten or humidify them later.

Small Collections of Wet Photographs, Negatives, and Microfilm

- Hang to dry. Use plastic clothespins on monofilament to dry negatives, post-1950 photographs, and microfiche.
- Reprocess all motion picture film and most silver halide microfilm to reestablish the correct chemical balance.

Slides

- Remove from mounts to prevent warping of image and mold and mildew growth under frames. Cardboard mounts are susceptible to warping and distorting when drying. It is easier to remount than deal with the side effects of warped slides. Transfer the intellectual information from the slide mounts before discarding the water-damaged mounts.

Magnetic Tape—Handling and Drying Methods

This is one of the newest fields of preservation and the most difficult to tackle in terms of disaster recovery. Two factors create this difficulty. First, magnetic materials are very fragile and susceptible to external damage. Second, special equipment is necessary to copy the original and to determine if the data are intact. Of all the different formats and materials, the least information is available on recovering damaged AV materials. Research examining the preservation issues and stabilization of magnetic media is starting to be conducted.

Magnetic tape was developed after World War II and became an industry standard for instantaneous recording of sound. The industry branched out in the last 30 years to create audiotape and videotape, both reel-to-reel and in cassettes. Computer tapes and computer diskettes came later and are now quite common.

Computer diskettes are now found in all areas and departments of libraries and other cultural institutions. They are the most forgotten aspect and information resource when organizations are creating disaster response and recovery plans. Yet diskettes contain important day-to-day records of the business aspects of the institution, including payroll and invoicing. Magnetic tapes may contain the OPAC, internal circulation, and cataloging systems, as well as databases. Software may have been modified to the needs of the institution and may be difficult to reproduce. Documentation may be in paper or computerized form. When a disaster strikes, this information is usually needed for the business side of the institution to survive.

Much has been written by contingency planners on how to get the data up and running.[2] However, when it comes to drying, cleaning, and reading the damaged data, little information is available to help deal with the situation.

All magnetic tapes are composed of three layers of different materials—the base, the binder, and the emulsion—just as film-based materials are. The base is either polyester or acetate. Both are fairly stable and have their own unique preservation and deterioration problems. You differentiate between polyester and acetate in the following manner: polyester stretches when pulled; acetate breaks cleanly. There is sometimes an antistatic back coating, which can cause its own preservation problems when it becomes brittle or ages at a different rate than the base. The binder is often urethane. It holds the layer that has the signal embedded in it. The binder layer adheres the signal or emulsion layer to the base. The signal is encoded by magnetizing the oxides.

The major difference between videotape, audiotape, and computer tape is the way the information is encoded into the magnetized oxide particles. Each AV format must be played on the appropriate equipment to decipher and read the data. Because of the rapid development of these media, recording and playback equipment becomes obsolete quickly. After a few years, it may be difficult to obtain the equipment necessary to access the older data. Companies that specialize in the recovery of magnetic materials collect and maintain the old machines. Even so, recovered data should be transferred to the newest or most stable format available.

Magnetic tapes are sensitive to changes in the environment. Videocassettes and audiocassettes may last for years, accumulating little particles of dust and dirt until they are no longer playable. Before that point, the tape should be replaced or copied onto the same or a newer format. The life span for much of this material is approximately 10 years. By that time, the magnetic signal will deteriorate, the picture or sound will not be audible, or the tape itself will deteriorate. Poor storage and environmental conditions accelerate the deterioration of the tape and its magnetic signal.

The optimum or ideal environment for magnetic media is 50° to 60° Fahrenheit with a maximum of 30 percent to 40 percent relative humidity.[3] If this environment cannot be achieved, then strive for standard working conditions of 68° to 70° Fahrenheit with a maximum of 50 percent to 55 percent relative humidity. As with paper and photographs, a stable, constant environment is best. Fluctuations in temperature and relative humidity will exacerbate the deterioration of the components of magnetic tape.

Vulnerabilities of magnetic tape abound. Temperature and humidity cause all types of preservation and playback problems. High temperatures can increase the distortion of sound, data, or image, as well as the physical tape. High temperatures can cause sticking when winding and rewinding and encourage layer-to-layer adhesion. High humidity encourages the deterioration of the binder layer, shedding of the signal or emulsion layer, and clogging of equipment when the tape layers flake off.

On the other hand, temperatures that are too low can cause tapes to loosen on their spools and can change the dimensions of tapes, thereby encouraging distortion and timing errors. If tapes are cold or frozen, allow time for the tapes to acclimate to new temperatures before winding, playing, or repairing. Low humidity encourages the attraction of debris and dust particles to tape, increases static electricity on tapes and in machines, and inhibits playing of tapes.

Damaging Conditions

Magnetic tape is extremely sensitive to heat. Diskettes, film, and magnetic media distort and become unreadable at 125° Fahrenheit. Paper does not start to smolder until 350° Fahrenheit.

Frequent changes in temperature can cause oozing or a white deposit on the tape. Playing a tape with white deposits will damage the tape irreparably, as the deposits will stick to the play heads.[4] This white deposit must be removed by a professional. Do not attempt to remove it. Send the tape to a videotape or audiotape cleaning or restoration firm.[5]

Mold and mildew are also enemies of magnetic tape. Mold will eat away the binder layer, obstructing readability of magnetic signals and distorting images or signals on the tape. Care must be taken not to seal a tape in a plastic bag or container that does not permit air exchange.

Drying Methods

During or immediately after a disaster involving water, remove all magnetic media to a dry, secure area. Tapes should be removed from their boxes and containers to prevent mold growth and deterioration of the magnetic signal. If the tape is not wet, remove the tape to another location, being careful to retain the title or identifying information. Disinfect the containers, dry thoroughly, and let them sit 48 hours to prevent trapping moisture. Store magnetic media without boxes in a clean, smoke-and-particulate-free environment while cleaning the containers. Tape is extremely sensitive to pollution; this includes solvents, particulate matter, cigarette smoke, and dust. After the containers have dried, and been labeled if necessary, replace the tape.

If magnetic tape is wet, remove all excess water from the container and treat it as indicated above. Dry the outside of the open reels first. Cassettes can be opened and all external surfaces dried. Air dry all tape. If the tape is wound tightly and properly upon the spool, no water should be present between layers. The danger here is that moisture will cause the adhesives to release or the layers of tape to come apart. In addition, mold could begin to grow on the tape surfaces. Do not attempt to play tapes as a means of drying them. If there are a lot of tapes, a professional magnetic tape cleaning and restoration firm may be better suited for this cleaning project. Do not use tape machines to dry or clean tapes, unless they are designed to do so.

When all tapes and containers are dry, have the tapes cleaned professionally or on a special tape cleaning machine. One such machine is called an RTI cleaner and is available from TekMedia (see appendix B). It is designed for use with *commercially* produced videotapes only.

Unique items or non-commercial videotapes should be identified during the prioritization phase and ranked for recovery. Clean and transfer water-damaged or moldy magnetic tapes by contracting with a conservator or professional specializing in magnetic tape. Commercial and non-unique tapes should be replaced if they are water damaged.

Compact Discs (CDs) and DVDs— Handling and Drying Methods

As libraries, archives, and historical societies actively utilize advances in technology, CDs, DVDs, and optical discs in all their formats become more and more prevalent. Research on longevity and the effects of the environment has just begun. It is still not clear how long data, visuals, sounds, or signals will remain encoded on discs. The current estimate is at least 10 to 25 years if there are no severe scratches or nicks that would affect the encoding.

Information on preservation, environmental and storage needs of discs, and recovering water-damaged CDs and DVDs is still difficult to come by. Researchers are just starting to write about tests and real-life experience with this format. The lack of information is due primarily to the newness of this technology. CDs and optical video, laser discs, CD-ROMs, and interactive multimedia permutations are more visible in cultural institutions than 10 years ago. Preservation, handling, and recovery guidelines are still being developed. For DVDs the format and encoding are even newer, so there is even less information available. The industry is still looking at the physical longevity as 10 to 30 years.

CDs come in some of the following formats: CD-ROM (Read-Only Memory); CD-I (Interactive);

CD-WORMs (Write Once, Read Many times); Photo-CD (these are CD-WORMs with photographs encoded to various scales); and CD (usually denotes audio only). Optical formats include video or laser discs, which are 12-inch platters with visual images or densely encoded programming information; and optical discs, which come in a variety of sizes from 5 to 10 inches and usually contain office records with or without images. Three-inch compact discs are starting to be available. DVDs are also called Digital Versatile Discs or Digital Video Discs. According to the literature, DVD is not an acronym.

All these CDs are variations of the same format and should be treated the same way. It is important to note that, with the exception of optical discs, almost all CDs are commercially produced and should be replaced if not playable. Optical discs contain unique information and should be treated carefully. They are generally irreplaceable, and the print materials that were input to create the disc were usually discarded after scanning was completed.

All compact and optical discs are composed of five layers: the *label*, an acrylic that is often silk-screened onto the CD; the *sealcoat*, which protects the metal and pit layers; the *metal layer*, made of aluminum, copper, silver, or sometimes gold; the *pits*, which hold the encoded signals; and *polycarbonate* (substrate), which seals the layers together, preventing deterioration of the metal and pits and protecting the metal from scratches. The label layer is directly on top of the metal, which holds the pits. Thus, the label is the most vulnerable layer of the CD.

Optical discs and CD-ROMs that are encoded on both sides and are housed in cartridges are very vulnerable to damage. Do not remove them from their cartridge unless wet. Avoid fingerprints, smudges, and dust on the surface of optical discs. This can cause reading errors and distortions.

The physical difference between DVDs and CDs is that DVDs can be encoded on both sides. The DVD is made of two layers, bonded together to make a disc that is the same thickness as the CD.[6]

CDs are fairly stable and, for the most part, will remain unaffected by normal temperatures. For longevity and seldom used collections, optimal or ideal environmental conditions are 68° Fahrenheit with

45 percent relative humidity. As with all formats, it is best to keep the temperature and relative humidity stable. Fluctuations in temperature could cause the polycarbonate to crack. Avoid freezing compact and optical discs. CDs are also susceptible to high temperatures: the polycarbonate may soften at 100° centigrade.

All particulate matter and pollution should be avoided as they can inhibit the signal and erode the polycarbonate. *Avoid storing CDs near solvents, such as janitorial supplies, ozone, and paint; they will eat the polycarbonate.*

Damaging Conditions

Compact and optical discs are susceptible to water, mold, and mildew. If the polycarbonate surface is damaged or not sealed appropriately, moisture can become trapped and begin to corrode the metal encoding surface. If moisture or mold is invasive enough, it will make the disc unreadable.

Clean surfaces with dry, lint-free cotton cloth. Clean discs from the center out, using a motion that is perpendicular to the grooves to avoid damaging and scratching the polycarbonate surface. Disinfect and dry all wet or soot-damaged containers. Allow them to dry for 48 hours. Store discs in a dry, clean, pollution- and particulate-free environment.

Because DVDs can be coded on both sides, if they are water- or soot-damaged, extra care must be taken to remove the debris and dirt from the surface. Try not to touch the surface at all by handling the DVDs by the center hole and the edge. Clean gently as you would a CD.

Phonograph Records— Handling and Drying Methods

Modern LPs are made of vinyl or plastic that is flexible and fairly stable. Older phonograph records can be made of acetate, shellac, glass, metal, cardboard, or any combination thereof. They range in size from 7 to 20 inches in diameter. The most common sizes are 10, 12, and 16 inches. Records can vary within each size as much as ¾ inch and can be up to ½ inch thick.

The primary preservation issues to deal with are warping, mold from poor environmental conditions, scratches from abrasion, incorrect playback equipment, and cleaning.

Storing LPs

Phonograph records should be stored perpendicular to the shelf, with the same type and size stored together. Store records in paper sleeves or inert plastic sleeves. The sleeved records can be stored in cardboard record sleeves, boxes, or just in the sleeve. Try to avoid wrinkles; they can permanently distort the playing surface. Records are very heavy and can damage each other if packed too tightly on the shelf.

Environmental Conditions

- The ideal environmental conditions are 68° Fahrenheit with a relative humidity of 45 percent.
- Keep the environment stable.
- Avoid all particulate matter and pollution.

Water-Damaged LPs 1970s–1990s

The following seven procedures deal primarily with vinyl recordings. Recordings made before 1970 are more susceptible to damage from water, mold, and rough handling.

1. Remove all discs from paper or plastic sleeves upon exposure to moisture or water. This prevents additional growth of mold and mildew and decreases decay and damage to plastics and vinyl.

2. If discs are vinyl (1970s–1990s), clean and remove water with a clean lint-free cotton cloth. This cloth can be dampened with slightly soapy water (one teaspoon mild soap such as Ivory or Kodak Fotoflo 200 to 1 gallon lukewarm distilled water. Do not use tap water—it contains impurities that can create deposits of crystals in the grooves) or use LP Discwasher solution sparingly.

3. Move cloth in a circular manner counterclockwise along the grooves in the disc.

4. Clean both sides of the record gently and air dry in a rack so the discs are perpendicular to a surface or with a lint-free cotton cloth. Be certain the paper label is completely dry before placing discs in new sleeves.

5. Call a conservator if the LPs are not plastic or vinyl (that is, from 1969 or earlier).

6. Label record sleeves.

7. Replace records in new sleeves when completely dry. (Paper sleeves should not have plastic lining.)

Most vinyl records will not be damaged by a minimal amount of water. The greatest dangers to vinyl records are mold from not drying them thoroughly and that the labels might come off when exposed to water.

Cleaning machines could be used after the records are dry. The most common are made by Nitty Gritty Record Care Products and Keith Monks Audio Laboratory (see appendix B). Their machines use alcohol-based cleaners that remove dust, dirt, and mold. Alcohol-based cleaners (including LP Discwasher) should not be used on acetate and shellac records.

Works of Art on Canvas and Paper—Handling and Drying Methods

The following four steps must be taken when drying and stabilizing works of art on canvas and paper.

1. Contact an art conservator during the prioritization phase, when these items are identified, located on the floor plan, and ranked for recovery.

2. The paintings should be removed to a separate location to avoid any additional damage.

3. Paper backing should be opened and removed from any of the paintings that are wet. You can remove the paintings from the frames if the paintings are wet, allowing them to dry on all sides. Do not remove paintings from the stretchers. A conservator can flatten warped paintings that are mounted on stretchers.

4. Check the backs of these paintings for indications of mold or mold stains.

Discuss stabilization techniques with an art conservator before freezing or drying works of art on canvas or paper.

Mold

Mold is constantly present in the air and on most objects. It is most evident in locations where there is a high relative humidity or when there has been water damage. Its presence, particularly the smell, is sometimes masked by odors of wet items, such as acoustic tiles.

Mold should be treated seriously. It is highly infectious and will spread throughout furnishings, materials, and the building. Mold will irritate people who have allergies and asthma.

Mold and mildew will grow between 40° and 100° Fahrenheit when conditions are right. Mold likes a *moist* environment and the dark, as seen by mold in a refrigerator or basement.

Different types of mold like to grow on different materials. Some like trees and wood; others like leather or the glues and starch found in books; and others like gelatin and paper pulp. In most instances, a variety of mold species will be visible on a "moldy" object. Three major types of mold are found in buildings: allergenic, mycotic, and toxic. Most tests will reveal allergenic mold varieties. An example of mycotic mold is Candida. A toxic variety of mold is *Stachybotrys chartarum* also known as *Stachybotrys atra*. This type of toxic mold has been in the headlines for the past few years.

Allergenic mold will trigger allergies and asthma. Coughing, sneezing, and discomfort are the most common symptoms. People working around mold, especially those with allergies, should protect themselves by wearing respirators, gloves, and disposable or washable clothing.

Working around mold can cause people to develop sensitivities and then allergies to the mold. Therefore, health and safety precautions are advised for all employees. In addition, all air in areas where moldy materials are stored or being cleaned should be vented to the outside. Air-handling systems should not be recycling this moldy air.

The presence of *Stachybotrys atra* is a sign that there is excess moisture or water within the building. It is sometimes found behind walls, sometimes in mechanical and HVAC rooms. *Stachybotrys atra* loves materials that are high in cellulose and it requires high humidity to grow. Not all black molds are *Stachybotrys atra*. If you do find *Stachybotrys atra*, consult with an industrial hygienist about testing and removal of the active mold. The source of the excess moisture should be identified and eliminated prior to initiating the removal of the mold from the building. Removing the mold without eliminating the excess moisture is pointless; the mold will just return.[7]

Control of the environment and moisture are key factors in dealing with and controlling mold. High relative humidity and hygroscopic materials will encourage mold growth. Hygroscopic materials include furniture, carpets, works of art on canvas and paper, textiles, acoustic tiles, paper, books, and wood. Moisture barriers are not always useful for controlling mold, for they may not let the moisture out, therefore allowing mold to grow. Examples of moisture barriers are vinyl paint, wall coverings, and plastic sheeting. The moisture condenses on the cooler side and encourages mold growth.

Effects of Mold

Cellulose or Paper-Based Materials

Mold eats away at cellulose materials, weakening the fibers and destroying the form. Paper becomes stained. Books will swell in areas where mold has infected them. Mold is attracted by an increased moisture content. Normal moisture content of paper should be between 6 percent and 8 percent. Below this, paper becomes brittle. Above 8 percent, paper is too wet and encourages mold to grow. Mold will grow on all areas of books and papers. Different species or varieties of mold are attracted to starch, adhesives, cellulose, leather, or cloth. Different colors and textures of mold indicate different species.

The goal of removing and "eliminating" mold is to keep it from germinating and thereby infecting

the entire collection or building. Controlling the environment and eliminating sources of "food" will inhibit mold growth.

Film-Based Materials

Mold is attracted to film-based materials such as photographs, negatives, microfilm/microfiche, and motion picture film. The mold will grow on the surface of photographs, etc., eating away the images.

To prevent mold growth, keep the rH below 50 percent. If mold starts to grow, clean off and store items under low rH conditions.

Mold also likes fingerprints and body oils and salts. Avoid touching photographs and negatives with bare hands. The mold will grow in traces of fingerprints and continue to damage the photograph surfaces.

If mold infects slides, remove them from mounts before drying and cleaning. Replace the mounts when the slides dry.

A method to prevent mold growth on film-based materials is to store them in frost-free refrigerators. Eliminate all sources of condensation in the refrigerator, or mold will grow without control. Store in low temperatures and rH. Use dehumidification if necessary.

The following are ideal temperature and relative humidity ranges for the storage of film-based materials:

Black-and-white film: 50° to 70° Fahrenheit (± 2°); 20 percent to 30 percent relative humidity, with a maximum of 50 percent relative humidity

Color film: 15° to 35° Fahrenheit (± 2°); 20 percent to 30 percent relative humidity, with a maximum of 50 percent relative humidity

Magnetic or Tape-Based Materials

Mold will infect magnetic and tape-based materials also. The mold is attracted to the binder or adhesive that attaches the layers of tape together. A white sticky residue is a sign of mold infection. Store magnetic and tape-based media in a low rH environment to prevent mold growth. Mold should be removed by professional tape restoration firms to prevent loss of image, sound, or information.

Controlling Mold

To control additional growth in a building and on a collection, determine what caused the mold.

- Check the temperature and relative humidity. The temperature should be below 72° Fahrenheit, preferably below 70° Fahrenheit. The relative humidity should be below 60 percent; the ideal rH is 45 percent to 50 percent.
- Dark, moist areas are prime locations for mold growth. Turning on the lights can slow growth.
- Check air circulation. Stagnant air and moist conditions will also trigger mold growth.
- Check intake, heating, and cooling ducts for obstructions to air flow.
- Check heating-exchange coils. This is a prime location for mold growth. Mold on the coils will spread throughout a building via the ductwork. Clean coils with disinfectant.
- Check air ducts. Clean any infected ducts. A fungicide or microbial cleanser can be used under controlled conditions, with approval by a conservation or preservation officer.
- Fix or eliminate the mold problem at the source. Treating only the symptoms guarantees another infection of mold.
- Isolate the infected materials in a room or area. Ventilate air to the outside to prevent spreading mold into the air ducts.

Change the Environment

- Increase air circulation and decrease humidity.
- Dehumidification is the best method. Opening windows if the rH is lower outside is a possibility.
- Measure the relative humidity using a hygrograph. Measurements should be taken several times a day. A hygrograph is the best instrument because it records temperature and rH over a period of one week or month and will provide justification for fixing serious environmental problems in a building.

Remove mold from books and objects. Vent all the air to the outside, both in the area with the mold infection and where you are removing mold.

Clean and disinfect the room, shelves, and any wood or metal containers. Use Lysol, Clorox, or a disinfectant. Try not to reinfect air ducts. Use protective clothing, gloves, and respirators when cleaning. Clean all clothing after exposure to mold.

Odors can be removed by opening baking soda or placing charcoal in the room. Do not use these items directly on books!

Ozone is not suitable for eradication or control of mold because of its side effects and unpredictability. See the materials on ozone, later in this section.

Cleaning Dirty and Moldy Books

Dry all materials before cleaning. Moldy materials that cannot be treated immediately should be frozen. Freezing mold does not kill or eradicate it but merely stops mold growth. Take the following six steps to clean dirty and moldy books.

1. Hold book shut at front edge.
2. Vacuum mold from
   - top edge of book, moving from spine to edge;
   - bottom edge from spine to edge; and
   - front edge from top to bottom.
3. Vacuum
   - front cover,
   - back cover, and
   - spine.
4. Open front cover.
   - vacuum inner edge near fold (hinge area).
5. Open back cover.
   - vacuum inner edge near fold (hinge area).
6. Repeat the process using a "dry chemical sponge."

Dry chemical sponges are made of pure latex or rubber, *not cellulose*. Do not get dry chemical sponges wet. Do not use any liquid to eliminate mold; *it will cause mold to grow again*. Do not put treated materials into sealed containers, boxes, or plastic; *this can encourage mold growth*.

Before returning cleaned materials to the regular collection, take the following steps:

- Look through the books and make certain no mold, soot, and dirt remains.
- Put books in a stable, dry environment.
- Monitor books for reappearance of mold.
- Return books to their original location after the environment is stable and the relative humidity is back to 45 percent to 60 percent (± 2 percent). These materials are very susceptible to mold.
- Monitor previously infected areas throughout seasonal changes to determine that mold remains arrested.

Mold in Buildings

A major cause of sick building syndrome is the presence of mold in the HVAC system. The mold is carried throughout the structure by the fans blowing air across a moldy condensation coil, heat exchange coil, or even moldy ducts. This contaminated air is recirculated again and again until it becomes a serious health issue.

External walls and joints contribute to mold growth. The moisture condenses near these cooler walls and can encourage the growth of mold. Keeping air flow active and increasing the temperature of the air near these external surfaces can control mold. Decreasing the moisture content of the air is also important.

Poor environmental conditions are perfect for encouraging mold growth. When a building is air-conditioned, there is a good chance for mold. Just because there is air-conditioning does not mean that there is humidity control. If the air-conditioning is up too high, surfaces can become too cold and the moisture content too high. At this point, water will condense on the surfaces and encourage mold growth. To prevent this, decrease the number of "cold" spots by increasing the air flow and the temperature.

Condensation on windows is a key indicator of an imbalance in the environment. Conditions are ripe for a mold infection.

Check air ducts, heating and cooling ducts, and intake ducts to make certain air flow is not obstructed.

Treat the cause *and* the symptoms, not just the symptoms, of poor indoor air quality.

- Clean all infected areas.
- Eliminate outside and building factors that encourage mold or condensation.
- Stabilize the environment.
- Monitor areas for reinfection.

Ozone

Effects on Materials in Cultural Institutions and Uses for Disaster Recovery

In the aftermath of the Mississippi River flood in the Midwest in 1993, and during several mold eradication jobs, a number of inquiries were made about the effects of ozone and what it can and cannot do.

Since 1993, there are some new studies on the effects of ozone on natural, organic, and cellulose materials, as well as on people. Most research on ozone examines its effects on the atmosphere. The creation and use of ozone indoors, and its side effects, were researched before the 1980s. Some of the new studies look at the effects of ozone during disaster recovery and in conjunction with indoor air/environmental quality. Ozone-generating machines, also described as "energized oxygen" and "pure air" machines are sometimes used to eliminate odors from soot-, fire-, or mold-damaged cellulose materials. This includes all paper formats, textiles, art on canvas and paper, wood, and photographs. In addition, ozone's effects on film-based materials such as microfilm, motion picture film, and magnetic tape were examined.

Background

Ozone found in the atmosphere is a very stable and powerful element. It screens out ultraviolet light and absorbs some harmful radiation. Ozone exists primarily as a gas. It has a pungent odor, most noticeable when electrical appliances spark.

Machines create ozone by passing an electric charge through oxygen. This is what occurs in the ozone generators or precipitators. Ozone is also a by-product of photocopiers and laser printers. This ozone is highly reactive and, therefore, very unstable. The extra oxygen molecule looks for other molecules in the room to attach to and creates some harmful, highly reactive compounds that damage materials.

Ozone is normally present in the atmosphere in concentrations of .03 parts per million (ppm). However, when generated artificially in concentrations greater than 1 ppm, ozone is toxic to people and animals. Ozone decreases lung capacity and function, aggravates asthma, and irritates mucus membranes, causing coughing and chest pains and increasing susceptibility to respiratory infection. OSHA regulates regular exposure up to 0.1 ppm; exposure in short duration is permitted, up to a maximum of 0.3 ppm.

Some scientists use ozone's powerful oxidizing properties for sterilizing water and purifying air. Ozone can be used for sterilizing food, but "effective bactericidal concentrations may be irritating and toxic to humans."[8] Many disaster response/drying companies generate ozone and use it as a deodorizer. To date, no government agency has approved the use of ozone generators in an occupied space.[9]

Uses and Effects

Ozone is highly effective for deodorizing materials after a fire or mold damage. It actually seeks out and attacks the odor-causing molecules, changing their molecular composition and, thus, neutralizing the smell. Similar changes occur when sprays are used to counteract odors.

The problem with ozone that is generated is that it is highly reactive. This ozone seeks out unsaturated organic compounds such as soot, mold, and molecules that create odors and bonds with them. That means that the ozone changes molecular bonds and creates a new compound. Many of these compounds act as bleaches and are very caustic. When natural or organic materials are exposed to ozone, the inherent chemical reactions already going on inside the item will begin to accelerate. Even with minimal exposure, ozone ultimately destroys organic, natural, and cellulose materials.

Libraries, archives, museums, and historical societies are full of cellulose, natural, and organic materials. Most paper created between 1860 and 1980 is acidic. Chemical reactions occur constantly, causing the paper to deteriorate, lose strength, and become very brittle. When ozone is generated for use in deodorizing the cellulose and paper-based materials, it tends to bond with the reactive chemicals already present and accelerate the aging process. *Even a minimum amount of exposure to ozone will cause these materials to become more acidic.*

Ozone speeds up the invisible and deadly reactions in paper, creating more sulfur dioxide and hydrogen peroxide and accelerating the acidic process. Ozone will cause paper to turn brown and become brittle. Eventually, the paper will become so brittle it will flake to the touch. Preservation and conservation activities in cultural institutions are designed to delay and retard deterioration of cellulose and film-based materials. *Using ozone to eliminate mold and soot odors may eradicate all advances in preservation efforts.*

When ozone comes in contact with photographs and film, it is even more deadly. Ozone increases the rate of oxidation of silver, destroying the images on film-based materials. It reacts even more quickly with color film than black and white. In strong concentrations, ozone can cause the images to flake off the film. The chemicals that once interacted to create and stabilize photographic images bond with ozone to cause the photograph to continue to develop. The same reactions occur when microfilm and motion picture film are exposed to ozone. In addition, ozone will react with the materials that make up magnetic media, causing the layers to deteriorate.

To make matters worse, as mentioned earlier, ozone is generated by photocopiers and laser printers.[10] Although the output of ozone is filtered and regulated by OSHA, these machines should not be present in rooms where large collections of cellulose materials are stored, especially film-based materials.

Compact discs and laser or optical discs are also adversely affected by ozone. Ozone can bond with elements to create solvents that cause the protective polycarbonate layer to deteriorate, ultimately destroying the signal or data encoded upon these discs.

The five most disturbing issues about ozone follow:

1. There is no way to know what chemicals and molecules are nearby to bond with.

2. There is no way to determine what the ozone will make when it bonds with other molecules.

3. Ozone can bond to create toxic or carcinogenic chemicals, or it can be harmless and dissipate into the atmosphere.

4. There is no way to predict ozone's behavior.

5. Air flow, temperature, and bonding elements must be factored into the high reactivity and unpredictability of ozone.

Uses with Damaged Materials

Despite all the warnings against using ozone, some disaster response/drying companies use it. Keep the following issues in mind before authorizing the use of ozone.

- Ozone, as noted above, is incredibly effective for removing the odor from soot-, smoke-, and mold-damaged materials. The ozone actually seeks out and attacks these odors, creating new chemicals that are sometimes caustic and sometimes benign. Ozone does act as a bleaching and disinfecting agent.

- Ozone can be used to deodorize an empty building. Use in office buildings, factories, and warehouses is possible, providing the precautions below are taken. Do not use in buildings when people are present. The ozone should be evacuated completely from the building or enclosed area before people enter.

Ozone should *not* be used on any items of lasting value found in cultural institutions. In high concentrations, ozone may remove mold, but these concentrations are deadly for the materials. Ozone should not be used with cellulose materials, as it causes them to become brittle and decompose. Paintings, textiles, paper, film, furniture, and leather are all organic materials. Ozone is highly dangerous to use with these items.

Minimal exposure to ozone is recommended— *no more than three hours total.* Remember, it is not for use with cellulose, natural, organic, or film-based materials.

Insects and Pests

After a disaster, it is particularly important to keep an eye out for insects and other pests such as mice, bats, birds, and other small animals. If there is a break in the building envelop or a change in the environment, your institution may become infected with insects and pests. But insects and pests may be present even without a disaster, so when surveying the building and performing routine maintenance and housekeeping, keep an eye out for them.

Let's start with insects. The most common types of insects in libraries, archives, and museums are cockroaches, silverfish, book mites, and termites. They are attracted to damp places such as basements and mechanical rooms. Anywhere moisture might collect, insects and mold will not be far away. Insects like to eat the starch and adhesives in book covers and leave droppings on books. Termites will eat into paper and cardboard and make nests that are difficult to remove and will ultimately destroy the objects they nest in and damage the physical structure of the building. After a disaster that involves water, it is extremely important to stabilize the environment as quickly as possible and to remove any standing water. Most insects like environments between 68° and 86° Fahrenheit and relative humidity between 60 and 80 percent.[11] Control of the environment and good housekeeping are the keys to controlling insects, just as you control mold growth. Use of insecticides, fumigants, and other chemicals should be the last control method you select.

The small animals, such as field mice, birds, and bats may come inside because it is warm and there are great nesting materials in paper, books, and boxes. You are most likely to find birds and bats in an attic; mice and other rodents in basements, loading docks, and other sheltered areas of a building. When you survey the physical building, look for evidence of pests and have a professional eliminate them and their access to the building.

CASE STUDY FIVE

Lessons to Learn By:
How the Financial Institutions Survived 9-11

Spurred on by the bombing of the World Trade Center in 1993 as well as other disasters where loss of computers was involved, many financial institutions began to plan for the worst. Financial institutions are required to have some type of contingency plan to get their data back up within 72 hours. Some businesses have set up "data mirroring" sites. Data mirroring echoes data recorded at other locations. In other words, when one key stroke occurs in New York, the same key stroke is made in London or Los Angeles, usually nanoseconds apart. This type of computer backup system has existed in the airline industry for years. Now businesses that execute hundreds of financial transactions a minute or hour have these "data mirroring sites."[12] Paul Kirvan, in "NYBOT Recovers with Backup Trading Floor" (*Contingency Planning & Management* (January/February 2002): 49–50), describes the history of the New York Board of Trade's contingency plan. In 1995/1996, the New York Board of Trade set up data mirroring with voice and data communications in a remote location capable of handling hundreds of traders and their support staff should a disaster occur. When the Center was destroyed on September 11, 2001, the New York Board of Trade (NYBOT) activated its plan and called on the telecommunications industry to set up and install the thousands of phone and data lines needed to get it back up by September 17, 2001. By September 24, everything was back to normal in the remote location.

Merrill Lynch was located across the street from the World Trade Center. When the buildings were hit, the 9,000 staff members were quickly evacuated and sent to the backup locations. Merrill Lynch had established an emergency command center in their New Jersey offices. The Information Systems staff switched all services to that location and distributed employees throughout offices in the New York/New Jersey area. Successful recovery is credited to extensive planning and, most important, testing. Merrill Lynch's plan was upgraded and tested extensively before Y2K. In addition to moving staff and operations, the company offered counseling and assistance to all those affected emotionally by the bombing and destruction of the World Trade Center.[13]

When we look back at actions after September 11, 2001, in the business and financial world, we see that they were prepared to move staff and operate using data stored in remote and backup locations.[14] Some law firms and businesses had extensive paper records that will be painstakingly reconstructed using court and client records. No matter the size of the business, each activated some plan to get back into operation as quickly as possible. Some had extensive plans designed in the aftermath of the bombing of the World Trade Center in 1993, some in preparation for Y2K and potential computer crashes. Still other companies created plans on the fly with employees telecommuting using their laptop computers and branch offices.

On September 20, 2001, Bruce Craig, National Coordinating Committee for the Promotion of History (NCCPH), reported in *NCC Washington Update* 7, no. 38, that, by one count, in New York City there are 42 museums, 57 libraries and archives, and some 245 outdoor sculptures that possibly have been touched by recent events. The National Park Service reports that the HVAC system at Federal Hall is also full of soot and the structure may have suffered unspecified structural damage caused by vibrations when the World Trade towers collapsed. Like thousands of other buildings, Castle Clinton also is covered with concrete soot. The National Museum of the American Indian (located just a few blocks from Ground Zero), for example, is covered in a few inches of ash. Reportedly, the dust is granular and greasy and may scratch delicate surfaces. Untold number of books, delicate fabrics, historic photographs and prints, as well as art works may need careful cleaning and conservation.

And lest we forget that the Pentagon was also damaged, . . . As far as the Pentagon disaster is concerned, the curator of the Army art collection reports that at least three paintings have been totally destroyed and numerous other pieces of art located throughout the building have suffered some type of damage due to water or smoke.[15]

Several organizations are collecting information about damage and loss of collections as a result of September 11, 2001. Documentation efforts are being coordinated by the New York State Historical Records and Archives Board (NYSHRAB). Information and assistance are available at www.nyshrab.org/WTC/wtc.html and through Heritage Preservation at www.heritagepreservation.org.

What Lessons Have We Learned about Disaster Response and Contingency Planning?

- It is important to have a plan, any plan. There must be some notion of where staff will work, how data will be accessed, and how customers will find the employees.
- Testing is imperative. Test the data, test the recovery, and test the telecommunications.
- Activate your disaster response team and get the operations up and running as soon as you can. Activate the disaster response plan *now*.
- Provide emotional counseling and assistance to employees to help them deal with the crisis.
- Don't wait until the dust clears; call the remote location and declare that emergency. Some remote data centers had hundreds of businesses call with a "declared disaster."

Only time will tell how the businesses and financial institutions will fare. Statistics show that half may fail before the next year is out. The destruction of the World Trade Center has strengthened awareness that any type of business needs a disaster response plan, libraries, archives, and museums included.

Endnotes

1. This should have been determined and the collections identified during the prioritization for recovery phase.

2. Articles pertaining to restoring computer operations are found within the bibliography at the end of this book.

3. Jim Lindner, president of VidiPax, interview by author, New York City, 1994. For additional information, refer to the bibliography.

4. This is known as "sticky shed syndrome."

5. There is a list of companies that provide this service in appendix B.

6. Information about the structure and coding of DVDs was found at SANYO Laser Products at http://www.sanyo-verbatim.com/dvd/faq.html.

7. Information about Stachybotrys atra is abundant. The best sources for information are the CDC and the EPA. Several print and Internet sites are listed in the bibliography under "Indoor Air Quality" and in the general resources. In particular see the fact sheet from the CDC available at http://www.cdc.gov/nceh/airpollution/mold/stachy.htm.

8. "Ozone," in *McGraw-Hill Encyclopedia of Science and Technology*, 7th ed. (New York: McGraw-Hill, 1992), vol. 17, p. 435.

9. U.S. Environmental Protection Agency, "Ozone Generators. . . ." (Washington, D.C., 2001), p. 1.

10. Torben Bruun Hansen and Bente Andersen, "Ozone and Other Air Pollutants from Photocopying Machines," *American Industrial Hygiene Association Journal* 47, no. 10 (1986): 659–665.

11. "Integrated Pest Management," *NEDCC News* 8, no. 1 (winter 1998): 4.

12. Data mirroring is also described in the Contingency Planning literature as data replication. For more information on this topic, see Tom Flesher, "Special Challenges over Extended Distance," *Disaster Recovery Journal* (winter 2002).

13. Summarized from article by Janette Ballman, "Merrill Lynch Resumes Critical Business within Minutes of Attack," *Disaster Recovery Journal* (fall 2001): 26–28.

14. Business and financial actions are chronicled in the various newspapers and news magazines following September 11, in particular the business and news sections of the *New York Times, Newsday, Wall Street Journal, Time,* and *Newsweek* during September 12–17, 2001.

15. Bruce Craig, National Coordinating Committee for the Promotion of History (NCCPH), "Cultural Institutions Impacted by World Trade Tower Disaster," *NCC Washington Update* 7, no. 38 (September 20, 2001), available at: www.hnet.msu.edu/~ncc. Ruth Hargraves, project director, "Cataclysm and Challenge: Impact of September 11, 2001 on Our Nation's Cultural Heritage. Available at http://www.heritagepreservation.org/PDFS/Cataclysm.pdf.

Checklists and Forms

1. Elements of a Disaster Response Plan

This checklist outlines the four sections of disaster response planning and recovery. Use it to make certain all the components are accounted for. Add to this list or modify it to reflect the needs of your institution *and* your specific disaster response plan. Use the elements as the table of contents for your plan. Just attach page numbers to each section or category.

Make a basic response plan with phone numbers the first page of disaster response manual for easy reference and contact. Post the daytime numbers for the disaster response team at phones for swift response.

For a quick and dirty plan, use the checklist for the three response phases in conjunction with the list of activities in the introduction (see page 4).

Prevention

☐ Survey building and collection for potential damage and hazards. Check fire, smoke, and door alarms, and exit signs.

☐ Mark collections that are water and heat sensitive. Make certain they are stored in areas that have the least potential for destruction.

☐ Monitor indoor air quality.

☐ Examine remote storage facilities.

☐ Plan for construction and renovation projects.

☐ Create list of consultants and conservators who can deal with the damaged format (get alternative names).

Planning

☐ Select disaster response team and alternative staff members.

☐ Assign responsibilities for each of the response phases.

☐ Set priorities for recovery of each of the collections (by format, type, department, floor, or building).

☐ Plan for large and small disasters.

☐ Plan for damage to computers.

☐ Review insurance coverage and update as needed. Determine what is not covered, and time, situation, and money limitations. Set update schedule for annual review.

☐ Establish communications policy.

☐ Contact disaster response companies and consultants for walk-through and discussion of their roles in potential disasters.

☐ Work with facilities and security to discuss their roles during potential disaster.

☐ Education—train disaster response team; explain responsibilities to rest of staff.

☐ Practice response phases—evaluate plan and revise.

Response: Three Phases

1. Immediate response to notification that there is a disaster.
   ☐ Gather the team.
   ☐ Alert outside professionals of the disaster.
   ☐ Determine if the building should be closed and for how long.

2. Assess the scope of damage.
   ☐ Call in outside assistance.
   ☐ Organize recovery steps based upon prioritization (developed or assigned in planning phase).
   ☐ Set up communications—internal and external.

3. Begin to deal with items that fall into primary prioritization/recovery categories.
   ☐ Reassign/reallocate staff as needed.
   ☐ Deal with emotional issues.

Recovery

☐ Restore primary services—skeleton staff.

☐ Restore primary functions—skeleton functions with available staff.

☐ Return to normal—most staff back to regular duties.

☐ Evaluate response procedures and revise disaster response plan.

2. Disaster Response Team Contact Information

Name	Phone

Emergency Meeting Place is located at

_____

Alternative Operating Location

Street address:_____

Contact name and phone number:_____

Directions (or append map):_____

3. Emergency Contact List—Services

Institution's insurance company _____

Contact person: _____

Policy number: _____

Phone number: _____

Alarm or security company _____

Phone number: _____

Account number/Password: _____

Contact person: _____

Power company _____

Emergency phone number: _____

Account number: _____

Gas company _____

Emergency phone number: _____

Account number: _____

Water company _____

Emergency shutoff number: _____

Account number: _____

Phone company	Emergency phone number	Account number
Local		
Long distance company		
Voice-mail		
Cellular or pager service		
Internet service provider		

Information systems/specialist: _____

Phone number: _____

Computer vendor company	Phone number	Contact person

Office Space Rental Company_____

Contact person:_____

Phone number:_____

Location:_____

Office Suite/Services Company _____

Contact person:_____

Phone number:_____

Location:_____

Construction Trailer Rental_____

Disaster response service providers	Phone number	Contact person
Servpro Drying Company	1-800-909-7189	
Belfor USA Group, Inc.	1-800-856-3333	
Munters Moisture Control Services (MMCS)	1-800-422-6379	
BMS Catastrophe Services (BMS CAT)	1-800-433-2940	

4. Phase I Activate Plan—Gather Disaster Response Team

Activate emergency purchase orders and contingency fund

Document actions and expenditures

Insurance company contacted at _____

      Contact phone number and name

_____

      Claim number

Floor plans assembled and as built blueprints located. Contact person is

_____

Visual documentation by digital, film, or video camera.

Indicate areas to be photographed on Phase II—Assessment forms.

_____

_____

_____

Utilities shut off at _____ o'clock by _____

5. Phase II Assessment Phase—External Structural Damage

Documenting the Damage—Create One Chart per Building

Perform and document a building structure survey and collection survey noting damaged and undamaged materials. *(This should be updated daily for the first week, weekly after that.)*

External structure	Type of damage	Action ordered date	Contracted or self-performed	Estimated cost (PO#)/insurance coverage	Action completed date
Walls		Cover holes			
Windows		Board up			
Roofs		Cover holes			
Foundations		Protect from water			
Doors		Board up			

Alert security about structural damage and open doors/windows to guard/monitor.

6. Phase II Assessment Phase—Internal Structural Damage

Documenting the Damage—Create One Chart per Floor or Department

Internal structure	Type of damage	Action ordered date	Contracted or self-performed	Estimated cost (PO#)/insurance coverage	Action completed date
Carpets		Remove or dry all wet areas			
Ceiling tiles		Remove all wet tiles			
Curtains/Blinds					
Furniture					
Internal walls					
Plumbing					
Mechanical equipment					

Indicate damaged areas on drawings of floor plans.

Contact person and phone number for contractual work:

_____

_____

_____

_____

7. Phase II Assessment Phase—Contents and Furniture

Documenting the Damage—Create One Chart per Floor or Department

Equipment	Type of damage	Replace or repair	Cost (PO#)/ insurance coverage	Date of completion
Copier number				
Fax number				
Telephone number				
Desk number				
Chair number				

Indicate damaged areas on drawings of floor plans.

Contact person and phone number for contractual work:

_____

_____

_____

_____

8. Phase II Assessment Phase—Collections

Documenting the Damage—Create One Chart per Floor or Department

Department or type of collection (by shelf, row, or call number)	Type of damage	Replace or repair	Contract service or self-perform	Cost (PO#)/ insurance coverage	Date of completion
Books/Bound periodicals					
AV materials					
Artwork					

Indicate damaged areas on drawings of floor plans.

Contact person and phone number for contractual work:

_____

_____

_____

_____

Off-site storage location and contact information for collections:

_____

9. Phase II Assessment Phase—Computers

Documenting the Damage—Create One Chart per Floor or Department

Computer components	Type of damage	Replace or repair	Contract service or self-perform	Cost (PO#)/ insurance coverage	Date of completion
Monitor number					
CPU number					
Modem number					
Server number or node number					

Indicate damaged areas on drawings of floor plans.

Contact person and phone number for contractual work:

_____

_____

_____

_____

Off-site storage location and contact information for computers:_____

_____

10. Phase III—Rescue and Recovery Phase

List contractors and contact information for repair of external damage:

_____

_____

_____

List contractors and contact information for repair of internal structural damage:

_____

_____

_____

List contractors and contact information for storage of furniture, equipment, and collections:

_____

_____

_____

11. Phase III—Rescue and Recovery Phase— Assignment of Disaster Response Team Responsibilities

Responsibility	Team member	Backup
Moving collections		
Packing collections (supervision)		
Inventory of damaged collections (for drying)		
Inventory of stored collections		
Volunteers		
Communications and assignment of staff		
Liaison with contractors and insurance		

12. Phase III—Rescue and Recovery Phase— Reallocation of Staff within Building

Name and home contact information	Reassigned (list responsibility)	Hours to work

13. Phase III—Rescue and Recovery Phase— Reallocation of Staff outside of Building

Name and contact information	Where assigned (what branch or library)	Cost of salary or unemployment	Hours to work

14. Phase III—Recovery Phase—Returning to Normal

Visual inspection of external building structure was completed on _____

Visual inspection of internal building and collection areas was completed on _____

Return of equipment and furniture is scheduled for _____

Return and reinstallation of computers are scheduled for _____

Return of collections is scheduled for _____

Shelf reading, shifting, etc. are scheduled for _____

Library reopens for patrons on _____

Press releases for reopening celebration sent on _____ _____

Staff recognition for work on disaster response is scheduled for _____

☐ Documentation of changes in procedures completed

☐ Evaluation of efficiency of disaster response plan

☐ Revision of plan

15. Phase III—Communications

☐ Inform staff—library closed (change emergency line information)

    Where to report _____

    When to report _____

☐ Inform vendors and suppliers—Library closed

    Phone number _____

    Fax number _____

    ☐ Temporary location _____

    ☐ Do not deliver

☐ Inform public—library closed (change recording on library info line)

    Return policy _____

    Where to return items if at all _____

    Contact number _____

Press releases to:

    ☐ Radio

    ☐ Newspapers

    ☐ Television

16. Prioritization for Recovery Checklist

☐ *1st Priority*

- Valuable/permanent papers
- Irreplaceable items—rare books, etc.
- Artwork
- Cannot get wet—pre-1950 photographs, clay-coated paper
- Objects, etc.
- Circulation system

☐ *2nd Priority*

- Expensive to replace/repair—rare books/manuscripts
- Essential to workings/function of institution, library, or information center
- Core collection
- Masters of microfilm (should be stored off-site)
- OPAC/Computer services

☐ *3rd Priority*

- Supplements core collection
- Heavily requested items
- Government documents
- Indexes, major reference tools, CD-ROM indexes

☐ *4th Priority*

- Standing orders/annual replacements and updates
- Nice to have but not essential to mission of institution
- Duplicate microfilm/fiche—otherwise replace
- Items duplicated by microfilm/fiche—periodicals, government documents

☐ *5th Priority*

- Disposable items
- Items replaceable with other formats

☐ *Other Items of Importance*

- Computer files should be backed up daily, if not more often.
- Rolodex/contacts and colleagues addresses
- List of vendors and suppliers
- Inventory should be stored off-site. Copies on diskette
- Artwork inventory off-site, plus pictures if possible to prove provenance

17. Vital and Permanent Records Checklist

Indicate where these items are stored:

☐ Contracts

_____

_____

☐ Articles of incorporation, certificates, licenses, or legal papers

_____

_____

☐ Titles, deeds, and mortgages

_____

_____

☐ Stock records

_____

_____

☐ Bylaws

_____

_____

☐ Resolutions

_____

_____

☐ Ownership and lease papers

_____

_____

☐ Insurance papers

_____

_____

☐ Board of Directors'/Trustees' minutes in microform copy (should be stored off-site)

_____

_____

18. Recovery Decisions and Priorities Checklist

If there is no plan in place or the prioritization for recovery phase was not completed, the following are guidelines of how different materials can be stabilized and some basic treatments.

If collections are not wet, quickly cover the stacks with plastic to prevent additional water damage, increase the temperature and the air flow, and decrease the relative humidity. Remember to remove the plastic as soon as the environment is stable or move the materials to a dry location.

Paper[1]

- Plain paper
  - ☐ Attend to within 72 hours.
- Clay-coated paper, including thermal-fax and self-carboned paper
  - ☐ Remove from water and treat or freeze within 6 hours of exposure to water.

Microfilm/Fiche

☐ Attend to within 72 hours or
☐ Keep wet and send for reprocessing.

Motion Picture Film, Post-1950 Negatives, Slides, and Post-1950 Photographs

☐ Attend to within 72 hours.
☐ Hang to dry.
☐ Keep wet or
☐ Freeze quickly.

Pre-1950 Photographs and Negatives

☐ Contact photograph conservator before treating or freezing.

CD-ROM, DVD, and Optical Discs

☐ Treat immediately.
☐ Dry and clean appropriately.

Magnetic Tape

- Audio or Video

- If unique *and* wet
  - ☐ Treat immediately.
  - ☐ Remove from water.
  - ☐ Send for drying, cleaning, and copying.
- If not unique (commercial tape) *and* wet
  - ☐ Discard and replace.
- If not wet
  - ☐ Clean tape.
  - ☐ Place in dry, clean boxes.

Computer Tapes without Backup Copies

☐ Treat immediately.
- Identify:
  - ☐ Format
  - ☐ Computer type
  - ☐ Amount of space used on tapes
☐ Send for drying and copying.

Diskettes without Backup Copies

- Treat immediately.
  - ☐ Dry
  - ☐ Clean and
  - ☐ Copy

Hardware

- CPU
  - ☐ Dry, clean, and recertify.
- Keyboards
  - ☐ Replace.

---

1. After drying, paper may have expanded and will require additional storage space or rebinding when returned to the collection.

(continued)

- Monitors (depends upon value)
  - ☐ Clean *or*
  - ☐ Replace.
- Servers
  - ☐ Clean *or*
  - ☐ Replace.
- LANs
  - ☐ Clean *or*
  - ☐ Replace.

- Unique or obsolete hardware (depends upon insurance)
  - ☐ Upgrade *or*
  - ☐ Clean.

Office Equipment

- Fax, photocopier, etc.
  - ☐ Dry, clean, and recertify.

19. Paper Records Recovery Decision Checklist

Depending upon prioritization for recovery decisions, some of these items may be replaced with like kind or CD-ROM formats.

☐ Vital and permanent records
  - Must retain original or legal surrogate.[2]
  - Dry and clean.

☐ Daily and retrospective records and paper materials
  - Remove from wet location.
  - Dry and clean as necessary.
  - Pack file folders in document storage boxes.
  - Label boxes with contents and location.

For small quantities (less than 500 volumes or 10 linear/cubic feet)

☐ To treat in-house:
  - Decrease temperature and relative humidity.

- Increase air movement.
- Spread papers out or support vertically.
- Paper may curl and wrinkle when drying.
- Watch for mold growth.

For large quantities (more than 500 volumes or 10 linear/cubic feet)

☐ Freeze
  - Ship to freeze-drying facility as soon as possible.
  - May be directed to ship in refrigerator/freezer trucks.
  - Freeze-drying takes 4–6 weeks depending upon quantity of materials and amount of moisture.
  - Have mold removed if necessary.
  - Loose papers should be returned in new folders if needed.

---

2. *Note: Legal surrogates* are documents that are scanned onto optical/compact disc; microforms, or some xerographic processes. Check with legal counsel for the most recent court decisions.

20. Clay-Coated Paper Recovery Decision Checklist

Is coated paper wet?

If no
- ☐ Remove to dry location,
- ☐ Or cover to prevent getting wet.

If yes, is it a priority to recover?

If no
- ☐ Discard.

If yes
- ☐ Must attend to very quickly or it will become solid block.
- ☐ Keep wet until ready to interleave (up to 12 hours).
- ☐ Or freeze and then freeze-dry.
- ☐ Interleave with sheets of double-sided wax paper or freezer paper and
- ☐ Start drying procedures as soon as possible.

Note: Whether freeze-drying or dehumidifying, the success rate for coated paper is 50 percent.

21. Books and Bound Materials Recovery Decision Checklist

Valuable or irreplaceable?

☐ If no, consider replacing with newer format.

☐ If yes, pack wet books flat or spine down in one-(1) cubic-foot boxes, and

☐ Freeze to stabilize physical deterioration and arrest mold.

Standing order

☐ Wait for new issue.

Replaced on regular basis

☐ Discard.

Reference title

☐ Replace with new version or newer format.

Periodical

☐ If already own microfilm copy, discard.

☐ If no, purchase microfilm copy or CD-ROM or consider using document delivery service for low use items.

Indexes

☐ Purchase CD-ROM for newer volumes

☐ Dry and clean *or*

☐ If destroyed, purchase older volumes as needed.[3]

For small quantities or damp materials (less than 500 volumes or 10 cubic feet)

☐ Air dry or dehumidify

☐ Check for mold and clean as needed.

☐ Check physical structure.

☐ Rebind or recase if necessary.

For large quantities or wet materials (more than 500 volumes or 10 cubic feet)

☐ Freeze

☐ Ship for freeze-drying as instructed by company. (Takes four to six weeks to dry depending upon moisture content and quantity of materials.)

☐ Remove mold as needed.

☐ Check physical structure.

☐ Rebind or recase if necessary.

---

3. Some index producers have special "disaster" replacement prices for purchases or hardbound volumes. Inquire if needed.

22. Microforms Recovery Decision Checklist

Wash dirt off surface with clean water if necessary.

Dry
- [ ] Remove to dry location or,
- [ ] Cover to prevent from getting wet.

Wet duplicate, vesicular, or diazo
- [ ] Discard and replace using copy from master copy.

Wet original or master (should be stored off-site)
- [ ] If yes, recover.
- [ ] Remove from paper boxes or sleeves.
- [ ] Send film for reprocessing—keep wet during shipment.
- [ ] Hang fiche to dry.
- [ ] Place in new boxes and sleeves.

Wet jacketed fiche
- [ ] Remove from water and treat immediately or it will stick together permanently.
- [ ] Remove film from sleeves.
- [ ] Hang to dry.
- [ ] Insert into new sleeves or jackets.
- [ ] Label accordingly.

23. Software and Data Recovery Decision Checklist

Backup version in dry, safe location?

☐ Load software and data using backup versions.

Need original software?

☐ Send to be dried and copied onto new tape or cartridge.
☐ Load copied version into "recertified" computer.
☐ Import data.
☐ Discard the original.

Time to upgrade commercial program?

☐ Purchase new version of software or new format on CD-ROM.
☐ Load onto computer.
☐ Import data.
☐ Discard the original, out-of-date software.

24. Computer Equipment Recovery Decision Checklist

Check the recovery priority for equipment.

Dry

☐ Remove to dry, safe location.

Wet

☐ Check recovery priority.

Upgrade scheduled?

☐ Replace according to needs and insurance coverage.

No insurance

☐ Open covers.
☐ Do not let ceiling tiles, soot, and dirt drop inside.
☐ Let inside dry.
☐ Recertify equipment.

Fire-damaged

☐ Open covers.

Soot or dirt inside

☐ Have disaster recovery firm dry, clean, and restore and recertify equipment to pre-loss condition.[4]
☐ Replace parts as necessary.

---

4. These companies provide restoration and recertification of water, fire, smoke, and environmental contamination damage for hardware. For example, Belfor USA Group, Inc., 2425 Blue Smoke Court South, Fort Worth, TX 76105 (800-856-3333). See the listing in appendix B.

25. Checklist for Determining Drying Method

☐ Type of materials that are wet.
☐ Amount of time exposed to water or very high humidity.
☐ Quantity of materials that are wet or water-damaged.
☐ Value or restrictions on access.

If more time is needed to make decisions or raise money, freeze and store the materials. Check with a conservator before freezing:

- Artwork
- Pre-1950 photographic processes
- Leather or vellum
- Furniture
- Pre-1950 phonograph records and cylinders

Note: Do not freeze magnetic tape.

26. Environmental Conditions for Air Drying Books and Paper Files Checklist

Temperature

☐ As cold as possible

☐ No temperatures above 72° Fahrenheit
High temperatures will decrease the life of paper and photographic materials, causing irreparable aging and secondary damage, such as release of adhesives and distortion of bindings.

Humidity

☐ As low as possible

☐ Moisture content of paper should read 6 percent to 8 percent when dry. Very dry air can cause paper and film to become brittle.

For very hygroscopic materials such as leather, vellum, textiles, furniture, and framed works of art on canvas,

☐ Very slowly reduce humidity to prevent additional distortion and to prevent structural damage.

☐ Contact conservators who specialize in these formats before treating or stabilizing.

Before accepting dried materials back from the disaster response or drying company:

☐ Stabilize temperatures in the institution to prevent absorption of excess moisture and to prevent a mold infection, and clean the area and get it ready for shelving materials.

27. Current Suggested Temperature and Relative Humidity for Cultural Institutions

Ideal ranges for:

- Open stacks, public access areas: 68° to 72° Fahrenheit; relative humidity 45 percent to 60 percent
- Closed stacks and low use areas: 65° to 68° Fahrenheit; relative humidity 45 percent to 55 percent
- Black-and-white film and photographs: 45° to 60° Fahrenheit; relative humidity 35 percent to 50 percent
- Color film requires colder temperatures below 32° Fahrenheit; with a relative humidity of 30 percent to 45 percent. Check with a photograph or film conservator.

Maximize air flow to prevent mold growth.

Note: If the collection was exposed to mold in the past, then maintain a lower relative humidity to prevent mold growth. Monitor the collection regularly for mold infections.

28. Cleaning Books Checklist

☐ Dry all dirty, sooty, and moldy materials before cleaning or removing mold.

☐ Moldy materials that cannot be treated immediately should be frozen. Freezing mold does not kill or eradicate it, but merely stops mold growth.

☐ Hold book shut at front edge.

☐ Vacuum mold off
  - top edge of book moving from spine to edge,
  - bottom edge from spine to edge, and
  - front edge from top to bottom.

☐ Vacuum off
  - front cover,
  - back cover, and
  - spine.

☐ Open front cover.
  - Vacuum off inner edge near fold (hinge area).

☐ Open back cover.
  - Vacuum off inner edge near fold (hinge area).

☐ Repeat process using "dry chemical sponge" made of pure latex or rubber sponge, *not cellulose*.
  - *Do not* get the sponge wet.
  - *Do not* use any liquid to eliminate mold, *it will cause mold to grow again*.
  - *Do not* put treated materials into sealed containers, boxes, or plastic; *this can encourage mold growth*.

When the cleaning process has been completed, before returning the materials to the rest of the collection:

☐ Look through the book and make certain no mold, soot, and dirt remain.

☐ Put in stable, dry environment.

☐ Monitor for reappearance of mold.

☐ Return to original location after the environment is stable and the relative humidity is back to 45 percent to 60 percent (± 2 percent). These materials are very susceptible to mold.

☐ Monitor previously infected areas throughout seasonal changes to determine that mold remains arrested.

29. Checklist for When Materials Are Returned from the Contractor

☐ Have file folders been labeled correctly?

☐ Are materials filed in their original order in document storage boxes?

☐ Are cartons labeled with proper identifying information? Include name of institution, number of items, location taken from, box number, and type of material.

☐ Check contents against inventory sheets.

☐ Are items dry and clean?

Note: Contact disaster response/drying company immediately if there is a problem. Report to the insurance company immediately any problems with returned collections.

30. Building Survey Checklist

Fire exits
☐ Visible and clearly marked.
☐ Exit signs and doors not blocked.
☐ Alarms on the doors work.

Emergency and fire alarms
☐ Ring in the immediate vicinity.
☐ Ring throughout the building.
☐ Ring or light up in a central security office.
Security people call _____ in an emergency.

Emergency lighting
☐ The batteries work.
☐ The batteries were replaced on _____.

Fire extinguishers
☐ Locations for all were marked on the floor plan.
☐ Type was indicated on the floor plan.
☐ Fire extinguishers are checked on _____.

Fire alarm call boxes
☐ Locations for all were marked on the floor plan.
☐ Type was indicated on the floor plan.

Smoke and heat alarms
☐ Meet the appropriate needs of the collections in those areas.
☐ Alarms ring_____.

31. Fire Extinguisher Information List

Location	Rating: ABC or A?	Last Inspection

32. Remote Storage Facilities Checklist

☐ Owned by institution
  ☐ Map and directions with identification of main and auxiliary entrances appended.

☐ Collections owned by institution only?
  ☐ yes   ☐ no

☐ Shared/regional facility?
  ☐ yes   ☐ no

☐ Contact information for other institutions:

_____

_____

_____

☐ Entire building rented?
  • Name of lessor: _____
  • Emergency contact and phone number:

_____

_____

☐ Designated space contracted from: _____
  • Emergency contact and phone number:

_____

_____

☐ Specific liaison from the institution and phone number: _____

_____

_____

Building survey of remote storage facility:
☐ Sprinklers present
☐ Fire and smoke alarms
☐ Utilities
  ☐ in separate area
  ☐ run near or over collections
☐ Floor plan appended

Collection-type survey of remote storage facility:
☐ Low-use collections
☐ Archives and paper record storage
☐ Data and magnetic media
☐ All of the above
☐ What level is it prioritized at? _____

☐ Create floor plans identifying and locating the utilities, collection locations with their associated priorities for recovery, and emergency exits.

☐ Identify personnel who are familiar with the remote storage facility collections and the building layout. These persons should be able to gain access to the building after hours (usually the head of the remote storage facility and the second in command).

Head of remote storage facility and phone number

_____

_____

_____

Assistant and phone number _____

_____

_____

☐ Dates or frequency of inspection of the remote facility and the collections.

_____

_____

_____

_____

_____

_____

_____

_____

33. Computer Backup Tape Storage Facilities Checklist

☐ How often are tapes taken to "remote" storage? _____

☐ Record storage or data storage—off-site
- Where are tapes stored? _____
_____
- How are tapes stored?_____
_____
- Environmental conditions:_____
_____

☐ Security
- On site
- In transit

☐ Who has intellectual access to computer data? _____

☐ Who is authorized to have physical access to data? _____

☐ Contact procedures
- 1-hour retrieval_____
- 24-hour retrieval_____

☐ Last visit to storage facility _____
_____

☐ Record storage or data storage—in the building
- Where are tapes stored? _____
_____
- How are tapes stored?_____
_____
- Environmental conditions:_____
_____

☐ Security?   ☐ yes ☐ no
Emergency phone number_____
_____

☐ Who has intellectual access to data?_____
_____

☐ Who has physical access to data?_____
_____

☐ Alarm system
- Smoke
- Fire
- Water

☐ Fireproof cabinets
- Rating _____

34. Telecommunications and Phone-Dependent Services Checklist

Fax

☐ Set up an account with a service provider.

☐ Use e-mail if available.

Voice and e-mail

☐ Write out routines on how to access the various information providers from an outside number on switchboard.

☐ Determine when each department is scheduled to have its system backed up and accessible (based on prioritization for recovery).

☐ Inform customers, colleagues, and suppliers of new fax and modem phone numbers or e-mail address.

☐ Designate one or two lines for incoming calls.

Internet service provider

☐ Write down user name, phone number for office, dial-up access, and technical support.

☐ Outline dial-up access procedures including configuring browser and e-mail service.

☐ Define who has access to change and move Internet accounts.

Website host

☐ Write out account, e-mail, and URL access information.

☐ Define who has access to change and move website.

☐ Provide phone number for Web developer, Web hosting service.

Modem

☐ Write out simple instructions for use without preprogrammed scripts.

- Cable modem (DSL and ISDN lines if applicable)

    ☐ Retrieve copy of operating software with drivers.

    ☐ Reinstall software.

35. Computers and Data—Hardware Checklist

Create a separate list for each system or location

For replacement and insurance purposes, keep track of what equipment is where.

Location:_____

Phone number:_____

ID or Serial Number	Computer Type (indicate if IBM, MAC, other)	Speed	RAM	Hard-Drive Capacity	CD-ROM

36. LANs and Servers Checklist[5]

Location or Department	Components	Network Type	Minimum Requirements	Serial Number/ Model Number

37. Modems Checklist

Indicate which computer stations attached to	Speed	Internal or External	Fax? If yes, speed	Model/ Serial Number	Connected to what serial or parallel port?

5. Include a diagram of how the LAN is configured, a list of essential parts, and a phone number for the service/ maintenance provider.

38. Printers Checklist

Location or department	Type (laser, ink-jet, or dot-matrix)	Model number	Serial number	Computer port attached to

39. Battery Backup or UPS Checklist

Location or department	Hours of power	Attached to which LAN or phones	Model number	Serial number

40. Software Checklist

Keep track of what is owned and where it is located for backup, replacement, and insurance purposes.

Commercial Software

Type of Program	Program Name and Version Number	Site License Number for how many stations?	Serial Number	Technical Help Number
Database program	Lotus approach			
Word processor	MS Word 6.x			
Windows				
DOS				
e-mail service				

Customized Software

Type of Program	Program Name and Version Number	Date of last modification	Documentation stored where	Technical Help Number

(continued)

Software Documentation

Program name	Location of backup program, diskettes, or CD-ROM	Location of manuals or documentation

Note: Not all computer software companies have a replacement policy for programs lost to fire or flood. Earlier versions are usually not available. Proof of ownership via serial and license number may be required for assistance.

41. Backup Routines Checklist

Suggested backup routines, off-site data storage requirements, hardware and software needs

Backup routines

- Method   ☐ full   ☐ incremental
- Frequency   ☐ daily   ☐ other
- Off-site storage _____
- Number of tapes per backup _____
- Second person trained in backup routine _____

42. Computer Backup Information Checklist

Indicate where each item is located

☐ Manuals:

_____

_____

_____

☐ Software licenses and current program versions:

_____

_____

_____

☐ Hardware configurations and requirements:

_____

_____

_____

☐ LAN configuration and requirements:

_____

_____

_____

☐ Data files (stored off-site):

_____

_____

_____

43. Online Services Access Checklist

☐ If the institution has an alternative working location or a hot site
- Store a current copy of communications software with log-on scripts.
- Install when computer is available; provide installation instructions.
- Add dial-up information for all hard-wired services.
- Change phone numbers for local access from remote locations.
- Confirm the system and configuration works.

☐ Does the institution have in-house online services?
- Provide dial-up access phone number, account number, and passwords.
- Outline search procedures.

☐ Keep a printout of the following with the program:
- Phone numbers for online services (voice, data, fax, and customer service) at the remote site
- Log-on protocols
- Account number
- Password
- Phone number for each online service's help desk

☐ Store, off-site, duplicates or the next oldest copy of:
- Manuals
- Basic access and search procedures
- Thesaurus for each online service

☐ Phone and account numbers for document delivery services

☐ Store, off-site, copies of phone directories for institution and local and regional consortia.

Associations, Organizations, and Companies

Associations and Organizations

Disaster response assistance and referrals

American Association of Museums
    1225 I Street NW–Suite 400
    Washington, DC 20005
    202-289-1818; fax 202-289-6578
    www.aam-us.org

American Institute for Conservation of Historic
  and Artistic Artifacts (AIC)
    1717 K Street NW–Suite 301
    Washington, DC 20006
    202-452-9545; fax 202-452-9328
    aic.stanford.edu/
    Request referral for conservators.

American Red Cross, Disaster Services
    National Headquarters
    430 17th Street, N.W.
    Washington, DC 20006
    202-639-3500
    www.redcross.org

Association of Records Managers and
  Administrators, Inc. (ARMA)
    4200 Somerset Drive, #215
    Prairie Village, KS 66208
    913-341-3808; 800-422-2762 (U.S. and
      Canada); fax 913-341-3742
    www.arma.org

Canadian Conservation Institute (CCI)
    1030 Innes
    Ottawa, Canada K1A 0M5
    613-741-4390
    www.cci-icc.gc.ca

Conservation Center for Art and Historical
  Artifacts (CCAHA)
    264 South 23rd Street
    Philadelphia, PA 19103
    215-545-0613; fax 215-735-9313
    www.ccaha.org

The lists in this appendix are not comprehensive; nor
does inclusion imply an endorsement.

European Commission on Preservation and Access
Royal Netherlands Academy of Arts and
Sciences
Kloveniersburgwal 29
P.O. Box 19121
NL-1000 GC Amsterdam
Netherlands
+31-20-551 08 39; fax +31-20-620 49 41
ecpa@bureau.knaw.nl
www.knaw.nl/ecpa/

Heritage Preservation
(formerly NIC—National Institutions for the
Conservation of Cultural Property)
1730 K Street NW–Suite 566
Washington, DC 20006-3836
202-634-1422; 888-388-6789;
fax 202-634-1435
www.heritagepreservation.org

Institute of Museum and Library Services (IMLS)
1100 Pennsylvania Avenue NW
Washington, DC 20506
202-6066-5836
www.imls.gov

International Centre for the Study of the
Preservation and the Restoration of Cultural
Property (ICCROM)
13, Via di San Michele
I-00153 Rome, Italy
oci@iccrom.org
www.iccrom.org

International Council of Museums (ICOM)
Maison de l'UNESCO
1 rue Miollis
F-75732 Paris
CEDEX 15, France
(33-1) 4734-0500; fax (33-1) 4306-7862
www.icom.org

International Federation of Library Associations
(IFLA)
P.O. Box 95312
2509 CH The Hague
Netherlands
+31 70 3140884; fax +31 70 3834827
IFLA@ifla.org
www.ifla.org

National Archives and Records Administration
8601 Adelphi Road
College Park, MD 20740-6001
700 Pennsylvania Avenue NW
Washington, DC 20408
866-325-7208
www.nara.gov

National Park Service (NPS)
1849 C Street NW
Washington, DC 20240
202-208-6843
www.nps.gov
Technical Preservation Services:
www2.cr.nps.gov/tps/index.htm

Northeast Document Conservation Center
(NEDCC)
Preservation Field Services
100 Brickstone Square
Andover, MA 01810-1494
978-470-1010; fax 978-475-6021
www.nedcc.org

Society of American Archivists
527 South Wells Street, 5th floor
Chicago, IL 60607-3922
312-922-0140; fax 312-347-1452
www.archivists.org

Special Libraries Association (SLA)
1700 Eighteenth Street NW
Washington, DC 20009-2514
202-234-4700; fax 202-265-9317
www.sla.org
Seek referral for a consultant to help rebuild
collections, computer systems, temporary
librarians, and online information providers.

Regional OCLC Service Providers

Preservation Programs and Assistance with Disaster Response Services

AMIGOS Library Services, Inc.
Imaging and Preservation Services Manager
14400 Midway Road
Dallas, TX 75244-3509
972-851-8000; 800-843-8482;
fax 972-991-6061
www.amigos.org

Northeast Document Conservation Center
(NEDCC)
100 Brickstone Square
Andover, MA 01810-1494
978-470-1010; fax 978-478-6021
www.nedcc.org

OCLC Online Computer Library Center, Inc.
6565 Frantz Road
Dublin, OH 43017-0702
614-764-6000; 800-848-5878 (U.S. and
Canada); fax 614-764-6096
www.oclc.org
OCLC provides some disaster response
services, including priority to get rewired,
reload data, and rent or lease computer
equipment to replace damaged OCLC
terminals. If the library is still using
catalog cards, OCLC will replace them
for a minimal cost.

OHIONET
1500 West Lane Avenue
Columbus, OH 43221-3975
614-486-2966; 800-686-8975;
fax 614-486-1527
www.ohionet.org

Regional Alliance for Preservation
www.rap-arcc.org/index.htm
Nationwide cooperative for preservation and
conservation.
Newsletter printed and distributed by
AMIGOS.

SOLINET (Southeastern Library Network, Inc.)
Preservation Services
1438 West Peachtree Street, NW–Suite 200
Atlanta, GA 30309-2955
800-999-8558; fax 404-892-7879
www.solinet.net

Water-Damaged, Film-Based Collections

Contact the organizations listed below.

American Film Institute
2021 North Western Avenue
Los Angeles, CA 90027
323-856-7600; fax 323-467-4578
www.afi.com/index.asp

Association of Moving Image Archivists
8949 Wilshire Boulevard
Beverly Hills, CA 90211
310-550-1300; fax 310-550-1363
www.amianet.org

Canadian Conservation Institute (CCI)
1030 Innes
Ottawa, Canada K1A 0M5
613-741-4390
www.cci-icc.gc.ca

Image Permanence Institute
Rochester Institute of Technology
70 Lomb Memorial Drive
Rochester, NY 14623-5604
585-475-5199; fax 585-475-7230
www.rit.edu/~661www1

National Archives of Canada
395 Wellington Street
Ottawa, Canada K1A 0N3
613-995-5138; 866-578-7777 (Canada and
U.S.); fax 613-995-6274
www.archives.ca

Northeast Document Conservation Center
(NEDCC)
    Preservation Field Services
    100 Brickstone Square
    Andover, MA 01810-1494
    978-470-1010; fax 978-475-6021
    www.nedcc.org
    Conservation treatment available from
       NEDCC and other regional conservation
       centers.

Commercial Companies That Will Reprocess Microfilm

Contact companies about specific services before adding them to your list.

Kodak Disaster Recovery Services
    Eastman Kodak Company
    1700 Dewey Avenue
    B65, Door G, Room 340
    Rochester, NY 14650-1819
    Attn.: Howard Schwartz
    800-EKC-TEST (352-8378)

UMI
    300 North Zeeb Road
    P.O. Box 1346
    Ann Arbor, MI 48106-1346
    800-521-0600 x2619
    www.umi.com

Magnetic Tape—Cleaning and Restoration Firms

Chace Productions
    201 South Victory Boulevard
    Burbank, CA 61502-2349
    818-842-8346; fax 818-842-8353
    www.chace.com/index.htm
    Sound and audio restoration

OnTrack Data International, Inc.
    9023 Columbine Road
    Eden Prairie, MN 55347
    952-937-5161; 800-872-2599;
       fax 952-937-5750
    www.ontrack.com and www.ontrack.com/
       datatrail/ (DataTrail Electronic Discovery
       Solutions website)
    Magnetic media, computer tapes, hard drives,
       and diskettes

John Polito
    Audio Mechanics
    6735 Forest Lawn Drive, #200
    Los Angeles, CA 90068
    818-846-5525; fax 818-846-5501
    www.audiomechanics.com
    john@audiomechanics.com
    Sound restoration and remastering

Tek Media Supply Company—A subsidiary of the
RTI Group
    4700 Chase
    Lincolnwood, IL 60712-1689
    847-677-3000 or 800-323-7520;
       fax 847-677-1311 or 800-784-6733
    www.rtico.com/tekmda1.html
    Cleaning, inspection, and repair supplies for
       AV: film, tapes, and discs

VidiPax—Magnetic Media Restoration
    450 West 31st Street–4th Floor
    New York, NY 10001
    800-653-8434
    www.vidipax.com
    Video; magnetic media; some film

Information Resources

National Center for Film and Video Preservation
    at the American Film Institute
    2021 North Western Avenue
    Los Angeles, CA 90027
    323-856-7600; fax 323-467-4578
    www.afi.com/index.asp

Water-Damaged Phonograph Records
Sources of Information

Association for Recorded Sound Collections
(ARSC)
    c/o Peter Shambarger, Executive Director
    P.O. Box 543
    Annapolis, MD 21404-0543
    (no phone given)
    www.arsc-audio.org

Christopher Ann Paton, C.A.—Archivist,
Popular Music Collection
    Special Collections Department–University
      Library
    Georgia State University
    100 Decatur Street, SE
    Atlanta, GA 30303-3081
    404-651-2477
    Sound recordings

Mark Roosa—Chief, Conservation Division
    Library of Congress
    101 Independence Avenue
    Washington, DC 20540-4530
    202-707-5213; fax 202-707-3434
    lcweb.loc.gov/preserve

National Library of Canada
    Recorded Sound and Video Collection
    Music Division
    395 Wellington Street
    Ottawa, Canada K1A 0N4
    613-996-7510; fax 613-952-2895
    www.nlc-bnc.ca

Steven Smolian—Smolian Sound
    1 Wormans Mill Court
    Frederick, MD 21701
    301-694-5134
    soundsaver.com

Seth B. Winner
    Seth Winner Sound Studios, Inc.
    2055 Whalen Avenue
    Merrick, NY 11566-5320
    516-771-0028; fax 516-771-0028
    Seth.B.Winner@worldnet.att.net
    Audio restoration engineer and archivist,
      sound restorations–classical music archives

Cleaning Machines and Supplies for Dry Phonograph Records

Discwasher
    c/o Recoton Corporation
    2950 Lake Emma Road
    Lake Mary, FL 32746-6240
    800-732-6866; fax 407-333-1628
    www.discwasher.com

Keith Monks Record Cleaning Machine
    c/o Digital Audio Restoration
    P.O Box 672
    Don Mills, Ontario M3C 2T6
    Canada
    416-444-3444 (10 to 10 ET);
      fax 416-444-3550
    www.audio-restoration.com/monks5.htm

Nitty Gritty Record Care Products
    4650 Arrow Hwy., #F4
    Montclair, CA 91763
    909-625-5525
    www.nittygrittyinc.com/index.htm

Mold and Indoor Air Quality Issues
Information Sources

Aerotech Laboratories, Inc.
    2020 West Lone Cactus Drive
    Phoenix, AZ 85027
    800-651-4802; fax 623-780-7695
    www.aerotechlabs.com

Environomics, Inc.
    3221 North 16th Street–Suite 106
    Phoenix, AZ 85016
    602-266-8288; fax 602-266-9355

Indoor Air Quality Information Clearinghouse
(IAQ INFO)
U.S. Environmental Protection Agency
P.O. Box 37133
Washington, DC 20013-7133
703-356-4020; 800-438-4318;
fax 703-356-5386
www.epa.gov/iaq

National Institute for Occupational Safety and
Health (NIOSH)
Education and Information Division
Publications Dissemination
4676 Columbia Parkway
Cincinnati, OH 45226-1988
800-35-NIOSH (800-356-4674);
fax 513-533-8573
pubstaft@cdc.gov
www.cdc.gov/niosh/homepage.html

U.S. Environmental Protection Agency
National Center for Environmental
Publications (NSCEP)
P.O. Box 42419
Cincinnati, OH 42419
800-490-9198; fax 513-489-8695
www.epa.gov/ncepihom

Disaster Recovery Companies

For local companies that remove standing water and
dry small areas in buildings, see the Yellow Pages
under "Fire and Water Damage Restoration."

Belfor USA Group, Inc.
2425 Blue Smoke Court West
Fort Worth, TX 76105
817-535-6793; 800-856-3333;
fax 817-536-1167
www.belforusa.com
Freeze-drying, cleaning, and mold removal
from print and nonprint materials, as
well as decontamination and repair of
electronic and mechanical equipment

BMS CAT
303 Arthur Street
Fort Worth, TX 76107
800-433-2940
www.bmscat.com/index.shtml

Commercial Drying Technologies
1520 Route 37 West
Toms River, NJ 08757
732-350-8036; fax 732-350-8027
Provides integrated water-damage recovery
solutions. Water-damage recovery/
restoration utilizing highly mobile/high-
volume desiccant dehumidification.
Service for northeastern United States.

Document Reprocessors
5611 Water Street
Middlesex, NY 14507
716-554-4500; fax 716-554-4114
www.documentreprocessors.com

Munters Corporation
Headquarter Region Americas
79 Monroe Street
P.O. Box 640
Amesbury, MA 01913
978-241-1100; fax 978-241-1219
www.muntersamerica.com

NBD International, Inc.
P.O. Box 1003
241 Myrtle Street
Ravenna, OH 44266
330-296-0221; 800-929-3398;
fax 330-296-0292 or 800-783-3802
www.nbdint.com
Water- and smoke-damage recovery of audio-
and videotape; computer tapes, diskettes
and CD formats; and vinyl records. Also
provides water- and smoke-damage
recovery of paper-based materials.

Servpro Drying Companies
575 Airport Road
Gallatin, TN 37066
615-451-0200; 800-SERVPRO (737-8776);
fax 615-451-0291
www.servpro.com

Contingency Planning and Response Companies with Hot or Cold sites

DataGuard Group, LLC
901 Fayette Street
Conshohocken, PA 19428
877-282-4873
www.dataguardgroup.com

IBM Business Continuity and Recovery Services
300 Long Meadow Road
Sterling Forest, NY 10979
800-599-9950
www.ibm.com/services/continuity/;
www-1.ibm.com/services/continuity/
recover1.nsf/documents/home

SunGard Disaster Recovery Services, Inc.
1285 Drummers Lane
Wayne, PA 19087
610-341-8700; 800-341-2688 or
800-HOT-SITE
www.sungard.com

Suppliers
Special Services and Products for Disaster Response and Prevention

American Power Conversion
132 Fairgrounds Road
West Kingston, RI 02892
800-726-0610
www.apc.com
Uninterruptible power supply, surge
suppressors

Blackberry—e-mail pagers
c/o Research in Motion
295 Phillip Street
Waterloo, Ontario
Canada N2L 3W8
519-888-7465; fax 519-888-7884
877-255-2377
info@blackberry.net
www.blackberry.net/index.shtml

Ebac Industrial Products
704 Middle Ground Boulevard
Newport News, VA 23606
757-873-6800; 800-433-9011;
fax 757-873-3632
www.ebacusa.com/home.html
Dehumidifiers—rental

FedEx Custom Critical
(formerly Roberts Express, Inc.)
2088 South Arlington Road
Akron, OH 44306
330-773-3381 or 800-762-3787
customcritical.fedex.com/us/default.shtml
24-hour emergency trucking and freight
service

Iron Mountain Inc.
745 Atlantic Avenue
Boston, MA 02111
617-535-4990; 800-883-8000;
fax 617-350-7881
www.ironmountain.com/index.htm
Remote storage of data, archives, microfilm
and digital data, some disaster recovery
support.

Munters Corporation
Headquarter Region Americas
79 Monroe Street
P.O. Box 640
Amesbury, MA 01913
978-241-1100; fax 978-241-1219
www.muntersamerica.com
Dehumidifiers—rental

ProText, Inc.
  3515 Leland Street
  Bethesda, MD 20815
  301-320-7231
  www.protext.net
  Boxes, supplies, and ready-made kits for
    disaster recovery

Remote Backup Systems, Inc.
  315 Good Springs Loop
  Rossville, TN 38066
  901-850-9920; 866-522-2587;
    fax 815-461-0298
  remote-backup.com
  Remote backup services and systems

SafeWare
  6500 Busch Boulevard–Suite 233
  Columbus, OH 43229
  800-848-3469
  www.safeware.com/index.htm
  Computer insurance

Servpro Drying Companies
  575 Airport Road
  Gallatin, TN 37066
  615-451-0200; 800-SERVPRO (737-8776);
    fax 615-451-0291
  www.servpro.com
  Local franchises rent dehumidifiers and floor
    fans.

VidiPax
  450 West 31st Street–4th Floor
  New York, NY 10010
  212-563-1999; 800-653-8434;
    fax 212-563-1994
  www.vidipax.com
  Videotape and film restoration

Basic Supplies

To get started and to keep on hand

  Plastic sheeting to protect collections and
    equipment from water
  Tape and waterproof markers
  Rubber boots and gloves for protection from
    water
  Flashlights with batteries
  Camera with film
  Office supplies: paper, pencils, pens
  Phone lists of staff and local assistance

Bibliography

10 Basic Articles and Books on Disaster Response

Cunha, George. "Disaster Planning and a Guide to Recovery Resources." *Library Technology Reports* (September/October 1992): 533–624.

Emergency Management Guide for Business and Industry. Washington, D.C.: FEMA, American Red Cross, et al. 1993. Available at http://www.fema.gov/library/bizindst.pdf.

Federal Emergency Management Agency (FEMA). Emergency Management Guide for Business and Industry. Washington, D.C.: FEMA. 1996. Available at http://www.fema.gov/library/bizindex.htm.

Fortson, Judith. *Disaster Planning and Recovery: A How-to-Do-It Manual for Librarians and Archivists.* How-to-Do-It Manuals for Libraries, no. 11. Edited by Bill Katz. New York: Neal-Schuman, 1992.

Kahn, Miriam. *Disaster Prevention and Response for Special Libraries: An Information Kit.* Washington, D.C.: Special Libraries Association, 1995. (Note: The print version is no longer available from SLA. It is available in full text at http://www.sla.org/content/Help/webcomms/sept11help/disip/infokit.cfm).

New York State Program for the Conservation and Preservation of Library Research Materials. *Disaster Preparedness: Planning Resource Packet.* Albany, N.Y.: University of the State of New York, State Education Department, New York State Library Division of Library Development, 1988.

Preservation of Library and Archival Materials: A Manual. 3rd ed. Edited by Sherelyn Ogden. Andover, Mass.: Northeast Document Conservation Center, 1999. See, especially, the section on emergency management. Available at http://www.nedcc.org/plam3/manhome.htm.

Price, Lois Olcott. *Mold.* CCAHA Technical Series, no. 1. Philadelphia, Pa.: Conservation Center for Art and Historical Artifacts, 1993–1996. Select publications available at http://www.ccaha.org.

A Primer on Disaster Preparedness, Management, and Response: Paper-Based Materials. Selected reprints issued by Smithsonian Institution, National Archives and Records Administration, Library of Congress, and National Park Service. Distributed by the participating agencies, 1994. Available at http://www.palimpsest.stanford.edu/bytopic/disasters/primer.

Walsh, Betty. "Salvage of Water-Damaged Archival Collections: Salvage at a Glance." *Western Association for Art Conservation Newsletter* 10, no. 2 (May 1988): 2–5.

———. "Salvage Operations for Water-Damaged Archival Collections: A Second Glance." *Western Association for Art Conservation Newsletter* 19, no. 2 (May 1997). Available at http://palimpsest.stanford.edu/waac/wn/wn19/wn19-2/wn19-206.html.

———. "Salvage at a Glance," the recovery decision chart that goes with the articles above. Available at http://www.palimpsest.stanford.edu/waac/wn/wn19/wn19-2/wn19-207.htm.

Audiovisual and Film-Based Materials

Care of Photographic Materials. Ottawa: Canadian Conservation Institute, 1996.

Fortson, Judith. "Microforms" and "Magnetic Media and Other Disks." In *Disaster Planning and Recovery.* New York: Neal-Schuman, 1992, p. 66–69, 70–75.

Hendriks, Klaus. "Storage and Care of Photographs." In *Conservation Concerns: A Guide for Collectors and Curators.* Edited by Konstanze Bachmann. Washington, D.C.: Smithsonian Institution Pr., 1992.

Norris, Debra Hess. *Disaster Recovery: Salvaging Photograph Collections.* Philadelphia, Pa.: Conservation Center for Art and Historical Artifacts, 1998. Also available at http://www.ccaha.org.photobul.html.

Reilly, James M. *Care and Identification of Nineteenth-Century Photographic Prints.* Kodak Publication No. G-2S. Rochester, N.Y.: Eastman Kodak, 1986.

Rempel, Siegfried. *The Care of Photographs.* New York: N. Lyons Books, 1987.

Wilhelm, Henry, and Carol Brower. *The Permanence and Care of Color Photographs: Traditional and Digital Color Prints, Color Negatives, Slides and Motion Pictures.* Grinnell, Iowa: Preservation Publishing, 1993.

Magnetic Media

Child, Margaret, comp. *Directory of Information Sources on Scientific Research Related to the Preservation of Sound Recordings, Still and Moving Images and Magnetic Tape.* Washington, D.C.: Commission on Preservation and Access, 1997. Available at http://www.clir.org/pubs/reports/child/child.html.

"Folk Heritage Collections in Crisis." Pub. 96. Washington, D.C.: Council on Library and Information Resources, 2001. Available at http://www.clir.org/pubs/reports/pub96/contents.html.

Paton, Christopher Ann. "Whispers in the Stacks: The Problem of Sound Recordings in Archives." *American Archivist* 53 (spring 1990): 274–280.

Saffady, William. "Stability, Care and Handling of Microforms, Magnetic Media and Optical Disks." *Library Technology Reports* (January–February 1991). Entire issue.

Van Bogart, John W. C. *Magnetic Tape Storage and Handling.* Washington, D.C.: Commission on Preservation and Access; St. Paul, Minn.: National Media Laboratory, 1995.

———. "Recovery Data in the Wake of Hurricane Marilyn." *NML BITS (National Media Lab)* 5, no. 2 (November 1995): 1, 8.

Zimmerman, Robert. "Shelf Lives and Videotape." *Fortune* (October 18, 1993): 99.

Information Sources

National Center for Film and Video Preservation at the American Film Institute, 2021 North Western Ave., Los Angeles, CA 90027, 213-856-7637.

National Media Laboratory, Box 33015, St. Paul, MN 55133-3015, 612-733-1110.

Compact and Optical Discs

Arps, Mark. "CD-ROM: Archival Considerations." In *Preservation of Electronic Formats and Elec-*

tronic Formats for Preservation. Edited by Janice Mohlhenrich. Ft. Atkinson, Wisc.: Highsmith, 1993. See, especially, p. 83–108.

Child, Margaret, comp. *Directory of Information Sources on Scientific Research Related to the Preservation of Sound Recordings, Still and Moving Images and Magnetic Tape*. Washington, D.C.: Commission on Preservation and Access, 1997. Available at http://www.clir.org/pubs/reports/child/child.html.

Mohlhenrich, Janice, ed. *Preservation of Electronic Formats and Electronic Formats for Preservation*. Ft. Atkinson, Wisc.: Highsmith, 1993.

Pohlmann, Ken C. *The Compact Disc Handbook*. 2nd ed. Computer Music and Digital Audio Series v. 5. Madison, Wisc.: A-R Editions, 1992.

Saffady, William. "Stability, Care and Handling of Microforms, Magnetic Media and Optical Disks." *Library Technology Reports* (January–February 1991). Entire issue.

Phonograph Records

Marco, Guy A., and Frank Andrews, eds. *Encyclopedia of Recorded Sound in the United States*. New York: Garland, 1993.

McWilliams, Jerry. *Preservation and Restoration of Sound Recordings*. Nashville, Tenn.: AASLH, 1979. See, especially, p. 22–43.

Nelson-Strauss, Brenda. "Preservation Policies and Priorities for Recorded Sound Collections." *Notes* (December 1991): 425–445.

Paton, Christopher Ann. "Annotated Selected Bibliography of Works Relating to Sound Recordings and Magnetic and Optical Media." *Midwestern Archivist* 16, no. 1 (1991): 31–47.

Pickett, A. G., and M. M. Lemcoe. *Preservation and Storage of Sound Recordings*. Washington, D.C.: Library of Congress, 1959.

"Sound Recordings" (special issue). *Library Trends* (July 1972).

Ward, Alan. *Manual of Sound Archive Administration*. Brookfield, Vt.: Gower, 1990.

Indoor Air Quality and Mold

California Department of Health—Indoor Air Quality Section. "Mold in My Home: What Do I Do?" *Indoor Air Quality Info Sheet*, 1998.

Chamberlain, William R. "Fungus in the Library." *Library & Archival Security* 4, no. 4 (1982): 35–55.

Northeast Document Conservation Center. "Security from Loss: Water and Fire Damage, Biological Agents, Theft and Vandalism." In *Technical Leaflet—Emergency Management*. Andover, Mass.: NEDCC, 1992.

Nyberg, Sandra. *Invasion of the Giant Spore*. SOLINET Preservation Program, leaflet no. 5, 1987. The updated version is at http://palimpsest.standford.edu/byauth/nyberg/spore.html.

Price, Lois Olcott. *Mold*. CCAHA Technical Series, no. 1. Philadelphia, Pa.: Conservation Center for Art and Historic Artifacts, 1993–1996. Available at http://www.ccaha.org.

Strang, Thomas J. K., and John E. Dawson. *Controlling Museum Fungal Problem*. Technical Bulletin, no. 12. Ottawa: Canadian Conservation Institute, 1991.

Thomson, Garry. *Museum Environment*. London: Butterworths, 1986.

U.S. Environmental Protection Agency and U.S. Department of Health and Human Services. *Building Air Quality: A Guide for Building Owners and Facility Managers*. Washington, D.C.: Superintendent of Documents, 1991.

Wellheiser, Johanna G. *Nonchemical Treatment Processes for Disinfestation of Insects and Fungi in Library Collections*. IFLA Publications, no. 60. Munchen; New York: K. G. Saur, 1992.

Ozone

Fink, Ronald G. "Ozone Uses in Disaster Restoration Business." *Disaster Recovery Journal* (spring 1998): 94–95

Thomson, Garry. *The Museum Environment*. 2nd ed. In association with International Institute for Conservation of Historical and Artistic Works. London; Boston: Butterworths 1986.

U.S. Environmental Protection Agency. *Ozone Generators That Are Sold as Air Cleaners: An Assessment of Effectiveness and Health Consequences*. Washington, D.C., 2001. Available at http://www.epa.gov/iaq/pubs/ozonegen.html.

————. *Mold Remediation in Schools and Commercial Buildings*. EPA 402-K-01-001 March 2001. Available at http://www.epa.gov/iaq/molds/index.html.

————. *Mold Resources*. (A list of resources and articles) Washington, D.C., 2001–2002. Available at http://www.epa.gov/iaq/pubs/moldresources.html.

Whitmore, P. M., and Cass, G. R., "The Ozone Fading of Traditional Japanese Colorants." *Studies in Conservation* 33 (1988): 29–40.

National Institute for Occupational Safety and Health. Occupational Safety and Health Administration. 29 CFR 1910-subpart Z.

Resources

Conversations with Professor Arnold Feingold–SUNY, Stony Brook, N.Y.; Professor Yair Zarmi–Ben Gurion University, Beer Sheva, Israel; Professor Robert Dezafra–SUNY, Stony Brook, N.Y.; Larry Wood–Disaster Recovery Services, Ft. Worth, Texas; Rick Kemper–Aegis Environmental Management Inc., Cincinnati, Ohio; Vernon Will–Ohio Historical Society, Columbus, OH; Doug Nishimura–Image Permanence Institute, Rochester, N.Y.

Computers—Digital Information

Hunter, Gregory. *Preserving Digital Information*. New York: Neal-Schuman, 2000.

Moore, Reagan, Arcot Rajasekar, and Richard Marciano. *Collection-Based Persistent Archives*. San Diego Supercomputing Center. Available at http://www.sdsc.edu/NARA/Publications/OTHER/Persistent/Persistent.html.

Selected General Bibliography

Alire, Camila. *Library Disaster Planning and Recovery Handbook*. New York: Neal-Schuman, 2000.

American Institute of Certified Public Accountants. *Disaster Recovery Planning*. Technical Consulting Practice Aid, no. 15. New York: American Institute of Certified Public Accountants, 1991.

American National Red Cross. *How Do I Deal with My Feelings?* Available in numerous languages at http://www.redcross.org/services/disaster/keepsafe/howdo.pdf.

Artim, Nick. "Cultural Heritage Fire Suppression Systems: Alternative to Halon 1301." *WAAC Newsletter* 15, no. 2 (May 1993).

————. "An Introduction to Fire Detection, Alarm, and Automatic Fire Sprinklers." *Technical Leaflet—Emergency Management—*Section 3, Leaflet 2. Andover, Mass.: Northeast Document Conservation Center, 1999. Also at http://www.nedcc.org/plam3/tleaf32.htm.

Bader, Nancy. "Run for Coverage: When Disaster Strikes, It Pays to Have a Plan." *Your Company* (summer 1993): 14–15.

Ballman, Janette. "Merrill Lynch Resumes Critical Business within Minutes of Attack." *Disaster Recovery Journal* (fall 2001): 26–28. Available at http://www.drj.com/articles/fal01/1404-04.html. *Note:* Online access to articles requires subscription to free trade journal.

Balloffet, Nelly. *Library Disaster Handbook: Planning, Recovery, Resources*. Highland, N.Y.: Southeastern New York Library Resources Council, 1992.

Barlak, K. "Emotional Coping Mechanisms in Times of Disasters." *New Jersey Libraries* 28, no. 3 (summer 1995): 13, 15.

Bates, Regis L., Jr. *Disaster Response for LANS: A Planning and Action Guide*. New York: McGraw-Hill, 1994.

————. *Disaster Response Planning: Networks, Telecommunications, and Data Communications*. New York: McGraw-Hill, 1992.

Bigley, Tom. "Backup for Safe Keeping." *InfoWorld* (October 15, 1990): 67–81.

Boudette, Neal E. "A Piece of the Rock for Computers: Recovery Firms Protect against 'Data Disasters.'" *Industry Week* (November 7, 1988): 85.

Burgess, Dean. "The Library Has Blown Up!" *Library Journal* (October 1, 1989): 59–61.

Byers, T. J. "PC World's Guide to Painless Backups." *PC World* (September 1990): 217–222.

Carlsen, Soren. "Effects of Freeze Drying on Paper." Preprint from the 9th International Congress of IADA, Copenhagen, August 15–21, 1999. Full text available at http://palimpsest.stanford.edu/iada/ta99_115.pdf.

Cerullo, Michael J., R. Steve McDuffie, and L. Murphy Smith. "Planning for Disasters." *CPA Journal* (June 1994): 34–38.

Chase, Deborah. "Disaster Recovery Systems: A Specialized Form of Insurance." *Inform* 3 (April 1989): 32–35.

Clolery, Paul. "When Disaster Strikes: Keep Your Practice Running." *Practical Accountant* 21 (May 1993): 24–28.

Coleman, Randall. "Six Steps to Disaster Recovery." *Security Management* 37 (Feb. 1993): 61–62.

Collingwood, Harris. "Message Therapy." *Working Woman* (February 1997): 26–29, 53, 55.

Conroy, Cathryn. "Accidents Will Happen: Formulating a Recovery Plan in Case of Disasters, Mishaps, and Hard Luck Might Save Business." *CompuServe* (September 1993): 30–33.

Cooper, Joanne Kimbler. "Sick Buildings: Some Fresh Remedies." *Business First of Columbus—Environmental Report* (May 17, 1993): 20A–24A.

Courtney, Philip E. "LA Earthquake Prompts Recoveries." *Enterprise Systems Journal* (March 1994): 98–99, 102.

Cox, Jack E., and Robert L. Barber. "Preparing for the Unknown: Practical Contingency Planning." *Risk Management* 43 (September 1996): 14–20.

Craig, Bruce (National Coordinating Committee for the Promotion of History (NCCPH)). "Cultural Institutions Impacted by World Trade Tower Disaster." *NCC Washington Update* 7, no. 38, September 20, 2001. Available at http://www.h-net.msu.edu/~ncc.

Davis, Mary B., Susan Fraser, and Judith Reed. "Preparing for Library Emergencies: A Cooperative Approach." *Wilson Library Bulletin* (November 1991): 42–44, 128.

Deering, Ann. "Online Disaster Management Resources." *Risk Management* 43 (September 1996): 12.

"Disaster Planning: A Necessity for All Firms." *Small Business Report* 12, no. 7 (July 1987): 34–41.

Dobb, Linda S. "Technostress: Surviving a Database Crash." *Reference Services Review* (winter 1990): 65–68.

Doig, Judith. *Disaster Recovery for Archives, Libraries, and Records Management Systems in Australia and New Zealand.* Wagga Wagga, New South Wales: Centre for Information Studies, 1997. (Available from: cis@csu.edu.au)

Ebling, R. G. "Establishing a Safe Harbor: How to Develop a Successful Disaster Recovery Program." *Risk Management* 43 (September 1996): 53–54.

Edwards, B., and J. Cooper. "Testing the Disaster Recovery Plan." *Information Management and Computer Security* 3, no. 1 (1995): 21–27.

England, Claire, and Karen Evans. *Disaster Management for Libraries: Planning and Process.* Ottawa: Canadian Library Association, 1988.

Ernst and Young, Entrepreneurial Division. "Hot Sites Help Firms Avoid Computer Meltdown." *Business First of Columbus* (March 15, 1993): 37.

Eulenberg, Julia Niebuhr. *Handbook for the Recovery of Water-Damaged Business Records.* Prairie Village, Kans.: ARMA International, 1986.

Federal Emergency Management Agency (FEMA). *Emergency Management Guide for Business and Industry: A Step-by-Step Approach to Emergency Planning, Response, and Recovery for Companies of All Sizes.* Washington, D.C.: FEMA, [no date]. Available at http://www.fema.gov/pdf/library/bizindst.pdf.

Fire Protection Handbook. 18th ed. Quincy, Mass.: National Fire Protection Association, 1991.

Fitzgerald, K. J. "Security and Data Integrity for LANs and WANs." *Information Management and Computer Security* 3, no. 4 (1995): 27–33.

Flesher, Tom. "Special Challenges over Extended Distance." *Disaster Recovery Journal* (winter 2002). Available at http://www.drj.com/articles/win02/1501-09.html. *Note:* Online access to articles requires subscription to free trade journal.

Florian, Mary-Lou E. *Heritage Eaters: Insect and Fungi in Heritage Collections.* London: James & James, 1997.

Fox, Lisa L. "Management Strategies for Disaster Preparedness." *ALA Yearbook of Library and Information Services* 14 (1989): 1–6.

———. "Risk Management for Libraries." *ALA Yearbook of Library and Information Services* 15 (1990): 218–219.

Gagnon, Robert M., P. E. Water Mist Fire Suppression Systems Theory and Applications. FireWatch, 1997. Available at http://www.nafed.org/Wmist.html. Hosted by the National Association of Fire Equipment Distributors.

Gallagher, J. N. "Preparation, Communication Are Key to Emergency Procedures." *Real Estate Forum* 51 (June 1996): 44.

Gauthier, Michael R. "Managing Information: How to Avoid a Computer Catastrophe." *Business Month* (May 1989): 81–82.

George, S. C. "Library Disasters: Are You Prepared?" *College & Research Libraries News* 56, no. 2 (February 1995): 80, 82–84.

Gibson, Steve. "To Keep Your PC Running Smoothly, Let the Power Flow." *PC World* (September 24, 1990): 32.

Gilbert, Evelyn. "Disaster Plans Called Key to Museum Loss Control." *National Underwriter: Property & Casualty/Risk & Benefits Management* 96 (May 4, 1992): 23–25, 50–51.

Gilderson-Duwe, Caroline, comp. *Disaster Recovery Supplies and Suppliers.* Madison, Wisc.: Wisconsin Preservation Program (WISPPR), 1995. (Order from: WISPPR, 728 State Street–Room 464, Madison, WI 53706)

Hall, Matthew. "Off-Site Storage Helps Firms Clean Up Their Act." *Business First of Columbus* (August 8, 1994): 17.

———. "Trade Center Offers Emergency Lessons." *Business First of Columbus* (June 7, 1993): 15, 18.

Hammaker, Robert, Robert Irvine, and Karl Brimner. "Managing the Mental Health Role in Disasters: An Alaska Experience." *Disaster Recovery Journal* (spring 1998): 16–22.

Hankins, Joseph. "Choosing the Right Automatic Sprinkler." *Disaster Recovery Journal* (April–June 1992): 56–60.

Hargrave, Ruth (project director). *Cataclysm and Challenge: Impact of September 11, 2001 on Our Nation's Cultural Heritage.* Washington, D.C.: Heritage Preservation and Heritage Emergency National Task Force, 2002. Available at http://www.heritagepreservation.org/PDFS/Cataclysm.pdf.

Harrington, Gary. "Flood! Or, Disasters Always Happen on the Weekend." *Southwestern Archivist* 16, no. 4 (winter 1993): 1–5.

———. "Flood Recovery in Oklahoma City." *Conservation Administration News* 54 (July 1993): 10–11.

Harris, K., and J. Fenn. "Emerging Technologies to Minimize Disruptions: Checklist." *Research Note Technology. Advanced Technologies & Applications* (September 2001). Available at http://www.gartner.com/reprints/backweb/101212.html.

Harrison, H. P. "Emergency Preparedness and Disaster Recovery of Audio, Film, and Video Materials." *IASA Journal* (November 1995): 82–85.

Harvey, Ross. *Preservation in Libraries: A Reader.* Topics in Library and Information Studies. London; New York: Bowker; K. G. Saur, 1993. (Contains reprints of articles and chapters)

———. *Preservation in Libraries: Principles, Strategies, and Practices for Librarians.* Topics in Library and Information Studies. London; New York: Bowker; K. G. Saur, 1993. (Contains reprints of articles and chapters)

Hendriks, Klaus B., and Brian Lesser. "Disaster Preparedness and Recovery: Photographic Materials." *American Archivist* 46, no. 1 (winter 1983): 52–68.

Higginbotham, Barbra Buckner, and Judith W. Wild. *Preservation Program Blueprint*. Chicago: American Library Assn., 2001

———."It Ain't Over 'Til It's Over: The Process of Disaster Recovery." *Technicalities* 16, no. 5 (May 1996): 12–13.

———. "Practical Preservation Practice—Managing Emergencies: Small Construction Projects." *Technicalities* 16, no. 9 (October 1996): 1, 12–14.

Hirsch, Steven A. "Disaster! Could Your Company Recover." *Management Accounting* 71, no. 9 (March 1990): 50–52.

Hoffman, Eva. *"Protecting Yesterday for Tomorrow."* National Association of Fire Equipment Distributors, 1999. Available at http://www.nafed. org/Library.html.

Hoffman, T. "Publisher Does Disaster Planning by the Book." *Computer World* 30 (May 20, 1996): 74.

"Hospital Cures PBX Failures with Surge Protection." *Communications News* (April 1994): 10–11.

IMUA Arts & Records Committee. *Libraries and Archives: An Overview of Risk and Loss Prevention*. New York: Inland Marine Underwriters Assn., 1993.

"Integrated Pest Management." *NEDCC News* 8, no. 1 (winter 1998): 4–5.

Jessup, Wendy Claire. *Integrated Pest Management: A Selected Bibliography*. Falls Church, Va.: Wendy Jessup, 1997. Available at http://palimpsest. stanford.edu/byauth/jessup/ipm.html.

Kahn, Miriam. "Mastering Disasters: Emergency Planning for Libraries." *Library Journal* 118, no. 21 (December 1993): 73–75.

———. *Disaster Prevention and Response for Computers and Data*. Columbus, Ohio: MBK Consulting, 1994.

———. "Disaster Prevention or Protecting Your Business." In *The RBS Book*, edited by Rob Cosgrove. Memphis, Tenn.: Data Precision Corporation, 1994.

———. "Fires, Earthquakes, and Floods: How to Prepare Your Library and Staff." *Online* 18, no. 3 (May 1994): 18–24.

———. *First Steps for Handling and Drying Water-Damaged Materials*. Columbus, Ohio: MBK Consulting, 1994.

——— and Barbra Higginbotham. "Disasters for Directors: The Role of the Library or Archive Director in Disaster Preparedness and Recovery." In *Advances in Preservation and Access*, v. 2. Edited by Barbra Higginbotham. Medford, N.J.: Learned Information, 1995.

Keeping Archives. Edited by Judith Ellis. 2nd ed. Melbourne: Thorpe in association with the Australian Society of Archivists, 1993.

Kiely, Helen U. "The Effect of Moisture on Paper." American Writing Paper Company, 1927. Available at http://palimpsest.stanford.edu/byauth/ kiely/moisture.html.

Kirvan, Paul. "NYBOT Recovers with Backup Trading Floor." *Contingency Planning & Management* (January/February 2002): 49–50. Available at http://www.contingencyplanning.com/article_ index.cfm?article=425.

Kuyk, Charlie. "Resolving Business Interruption Claims." *Columbus CEO* (March 2002): 39–40.

Laiming, Susan, and Paul Laiming. "Insurance: Minimizing Your Loss and Managing Risk." *Bottom Line* 2, no. 1 (1988): 14–16.

Learn, Larry L. "Diversity: Two Are Not Cheaper Than One! A Look at Facilities Disaster Avoidance." *Library Hi Tech News* (January/February 1992): 17–22.

Lemley, Don. "Precautions and Safe Practices for Records Storage Systems." *Records Management Quarterly* (April 1992): 24–27.

Lewis, Steven, and Richard Arnold. *Disaster Recovery Yellow Pages*. Systems Audit Group, 1994. (semiannual update)

Lull, William P., with the assistance of Paul N. Banks. *Conservation Environment Guidelines for Libraries and Archives in New York State*. Albany: New York State Library, 1990.

Marley, Sara. "Learning from Disaster." *Business Insurance* 27 (June 7, 1993): 3–4.

Maslen, C. "Testing the Plan Is More Important than the Plan Itself." *Information Management and Computer Security* 4, no. 3 (1996): 26–29.

Mayer, John H. "Disaster Prone." *Client/Server Computing* (October 1996): 47–52.

McCrady, Ellen. "Mold: The Whole Picture." Parts 1–4. *Abbey Newsletter* 23, no. 4–7 (1999). Available at http://www.palimpsest.stanford.edu/byorg/abbey.

Miller, R. Bruce. "Contingency Planning Resources." *Information Technology and Libraries* (June 1990): 179–180.

_____. "Libraries and Computers: Disaster Prevention and Recovery." *Information Technology and Libraries* (December 1988): 349–358.

Mitroff, Ian I., L. Katherine Harrington, and Eric Gai. "Thinking about the Unthinkable." *Across the Board* 33 (September 1996): 44–48.

Moore, Pat. "Safeguarding Your Company's Records." *Risk Management* 43 (September 1996): 47–50.

Morris, John. *The Library Disaster Preparedness Handbook.* Chicago: American Library Assn., 1986.

Murray, Toby. *Basic Guidelines for Disaster Planning in Oklahoma.* Tulsa, Okla.: University of Tulsa, 1985.

————. *Bibliography on Disasters, Disaster Preparedness, and Disaster Recovery.* Tulsa, Okla.: University of Tulsa Preservation Department, 1994.

————. "Don't Get Caught with Your Plans Down." *Records Management Quarterly* (April 1987): 12–41 passim. (bibliography 18–30, 41)

Myatt, Paul B. "Business Resumption Planning: An ROI Opportunity." *Enterprise Systems Journal* (November 1994): 83–88, 92.

National Parks Service. Museum Management Program. Dept. of the Interior. *NPS Museum Handbook.* Washington, D.C.: Government Printing Office, 1990. Available at http://www.cr.nps.gov/museum/publications/handbook.html.

Nelton, Sharon. "Prepare for the Worst." *Nation's Business* 81 (September 1993): 20–28.

New York City Department of Health. *Guidelines on Assessment and Remediation of Fungi in Indoor Environments.* New York: New York City Department of Health, Bureau of Environmental and Occupational Disease and Epidemiology, 2000. Also available at http://www.ci.nyc.ny.us/html/doh/html/epi/moldrpt1.html.

New York State Program for the Conservation and Preservation of Library Research Materials. *Disaster Preparedness: Planning Resource Packet.* Albany, N.Y.: University of the State of New York, State Education Department, New York State Library Division of Library Development, 1988.

————. *Environmental Controls Resource Packet.* Albany, N.Y.: University of the State of New York, State Education Department, New York State Library Division of Library Development, 1990.

Newman, William F. "Sky-High Disaster Management." *Security Management* (January 1994): 26–30.

Nichols, Don. "Back in Business." *Small Business Reports* (March 1993): 55–63. (case study)

Nishimura, Doug. "Fire Suppression Systems." *ConsDist.Lst* 20, October 1993. Available online in CoOL Archives at http://palimpsest.stanford.edu.

Nyberg, Sandra. *The Invasion of the Giant Spore.* SOLINET Preservation Program, leaflet no. 5, November 1987. The updated version is available at http://palimpsest.stanford.edu/byauth/nyberg/spore.html.

O'Connell, Mildred. "Disaster Planning: Writing and Implementing Plans for Collections-Holding Institutions." *Technology & Conservation* 8 (summer 1983): 18–24.

Olson, Nancy B. "Hanging Your Software Up to Dry." *College & Research Libraries News* 47, no. 10 (November 1986): 634–636.

Osborne, Larry N. "Those (In)destructible Disks; or, Another Myth Exploded." *Library Hi Tech* 27 (1989): 7–10, 28.

Pacey, Antony. "Halon Gas and Library Fire Protection." *Canadian Library Journal* (February 1991): 33–36.

Paradine, T. J. "Business Interruption Insurance: A Vital Ingredient in Your Disaster Recovery Plan." *Information Management and Computer Security* 3, no. 1 (1995): 9–17.

Pelland, D. "Disaster Management Reaches Mid-Size Firms: Planning to Survive." *Risk Management* 43 (September 1996): 10.

Post, Deborah Cromer. "Fire Protection Systems." *Security World* (March 1981): 30–32.

Ragsdale, K. W., and J. Simpson. "Being on the Safe Side." *College & Research Libraries News* 57, no. 6 (June 1996): 351–354.

Reilly, James M., Douglas W. Nishimura, and Edward Zinn. *New Tools for Preservation: Assessing Long-Term Environmental Effects on Library and Archives Collections*. Washington, D.C.: Commission on Preservation and Access, 1995.

Resnick, Rosalind. "Protecting Computers and Data." *Nation's Business* 81 (September 1993): 26.

Rightmeyer, S. P. "Disaster Planning; or, The 'What Next' Attitude." *New Jersey Libraries* 28, no. 3 (summer 1995): 3–18.

Roberts, Barbara O. "Speaking Out: Establishing a Disaster Prevention/Response Plan: An International Perspective and Assessment." *Technology & Conservation* (winter 1992–1993): 15–17, 35–36.

Robertson, Guy. "People, Paper, Data: Disaster Planning for Libraries." *Disaster Recovery Journal* 10, no. 1 (winter 1997): 38–43.

Rothstein, Philip J. "Up and Running; How to Insure Disaster Recovery." *Datamation* (October 15, 1988): 86–96.

Sanders, Robert L. "Planners and Fire Fighters: A Records Management Synthesis." *Records Management Quarterly* (April 1992): 50–59.

Seal, Robert A. "Risk Management for Libraries." *ALA Yearbook of Library and Information Services* 14 (1989): 218–221.

———. "Risk Management for Libraries." *ALA Yearbook of Library and Information Services* 13 (1988): 294–298.

Shelly, Rose Ann. "How the GSA (General Services Administration) Responds to Emergencies." *Communications News* (April 1994): 20–23.

Smith, Kenneth. "When Timing Is Everything: Disaster Recovery Timing and Business Impact." *Enterprise Systems Journal* (January 1994): 72–76.

Smith, Richard D. "Disaster Recovery: Problems and Procedures." *IFLA Journal* 17 (1991): 13–24.

Souter, Gavin. "Active Disaster Plan Thanked for Swift Recovery." *Business Insurance* 27 (June 7, 1993): 6, 10.

St. Lifer, Evan, and Michael Rogers. "Corporate Libraries Recover from Trade Center Bombing." *Library Journal* (April 1, 1993): 18–19.

Stagnitto, Janice. "The Shrink Wrap Project at Rutgers University." *Special Collections and Archives AIC Book and Paper Group Annual*, 1993, v. 12, p. 56–60. Reprinted in *Abby Newsletter* 18, no. 4–5 (August–September 1994). Also available at http://palimpsest.stanford.edu/byorg/abbey/an/an18/an18-4/an18-411.html.

Stephenson, Mary Sue. *Planning Library Facilities: A Selected, Annotated Bibliography*. Metuchen, N.J.: Scarecrow, 1990.

Stratton, Lee. "A Fungus among Us." *Columbus Dispatch* (January 6, 2002).

———. "Mold Causing Stink for Builders, Insurance Companies." *Columbus Dispatch* (January 10, 2002).

Sutherland, J. Warren. "Computerized Contingency Planning Can Aid RMs (Risk Managers)." *National Underwriters: Property & Casualty/Risk & Benefits Management* 97 (May 17, 1993): 11, 25.

Tanzillo, Kevin. "How Users Survived the 1994 L.A. Quake." *Communications News* (April 1994): 12–14.

Technical Support/Special Report: Disaster Recovery. Official magazine of the National Systems Programmers Association, October 1990.

Tillson, Timothy B. "Post-Disaster Recovery." *Small Business Reports* 15, no. 2 (February 1990): 46–50.

Tremain, David. "Notes on Emergency Drying of Coated Papers Damaged by Water." Canadian Conservation Institute, n.d. Available at http://palimpsest.stanford.edu/byauth/tremain/coated.html.

Ungarelli, Donald L. "National Statistics—Fire Losses for 1987." *Library & Archival Security* 9, no. 2 (1989): 50–53.

U.S. Center for Disease Control NIOSH. *Indoor Environmental Quality.* Document no. 705002. Washington, D.C.: Government Printing Office, 1997. Available at http://www.cdc.gov/niosh/ieqfs.html.

———. National Center for Environmental Health. Air and Respiratory Health Branch. *Questions and Answers on Cstachybotrys chartarum and Other Molds.* Available at http://www.cdc.gov/nceh/airpollution/mold/stachy.htm.

Van Mill, Susan, and Al Gliane. "Insurance and Disaster Recovery Planning: Business Income Coverage and Claims Preparation." *Disaster Recovery Journal* (spring 1998): 89–90.

A Virtual Exhibition of the Ravages of Dust, Water, Moulds, Fungi, Bookworms and other Pests. A general introduction to the topic, prepared by the European Commission on Preservation and Access (ECPA), n.d. Text and images available at http://www.knaw.nl/ecpa/expo.htm.

Vital Records and Records Disaster Mitigation and Recovery: An Instructional Guide. National Archives and Records Administration Instructional Guide Series. College Park, Md.: National Archives and Records Administration, Office of Records Administration, 1996. Available at http://palimpsest.stanford.edu/bytopic/disasters/misc/vitalrec/F.

Vossler, Janet L. "The Human Element of Disaster Recovery." *ARMA Quarterly* (January 1987): 10–12.

Walsh, Betty. "Salvage of Water-Damaged Archival Collections: Salvage at a Glance." *Western Association for Art Conservation Newsletter* 10, no. 2 (April 1989): 2–5.

———. "Salvage Operations for Water-Damaged Archival Collections: A Second Glance." *WAAC Newsletter* 19, no. 2 (May 1997). Available at http://palimpsest.stanford.edu/waac/wn/wn19/wn19-2/wn19-206.html. The updated salvage chart is available at http://palimpsest.stanford.edu/waac/wn/wn19/wn19-2/wn19-207.html.

Walsh, Elizabeth. "Fire Suppression Using Micromist." ConsDist.Lst 28, September 1993. Available online in CoOL Archives at http://palimpsest.stanford.edu.

Waters, Peter. *Procedures for Salvage of Water-Damaged Library Materials.* Washington, D.C.: Library of Congress, 1975.

Watson, Tom. "After the Fire: Everett Community College Library Is Back in Business." *Wilson Library Bulletin* (November 1988): 63–65.

Welch, J. "On-Screen Disaster Provide Vital Lessons." *People Management* 2 (May 16, 1996): 9.

Wellheiser, Johanna G., and Jude Scott. *An Ounce of Prevention: Integrated Disaster Planning for Archives, Libraries, and Record Centres.* 2nd ed. Lanham, Md.: Scarecrow and Canadian Archives Foundation, 2002.

Western New York Library Resources Council (WNYLRC). *Western New York Disaster Preparedness Manual for Libraries and Archives.* Buffalo, N.Y.: WNYLRC, 1995. Order from WNYLRC, 4455 Genesee Street, Buffalo, NY 14225-0400.

Wettlaufer, B. "Preparing a Library Disaster Plan." *Library Mosaics* 6, no. 6 (November–December 1995): 8–10.

Whiting, Rick. "Spoilt for Choice." *Client/Server Computing* (October 1996): 40–44.

Wilson, J. Andrew. "Fire Fighters: An Automatic Fire Suppression System Is among Your Museum's Best and Safest Forms of Insurance." *Museum News* (November–December 1989): 68–72.

Wolf, Alisa. "Wake-Up Call: Fire at the U.S. Treasury Building." *NFPA Journal* 90, no. 6 (November–December 1996): 52–57.

Journals

With regular articles or columns on disaster prevention and response

Abbey Newsletter
    7105 Geneva Drive
    Austin, TX 78723
    512-929-3992; fax 512-929-3995
    palimpsest.stanford.edu/byorg/abbey

Communication News: The Applications Magazine for Networking and Information Management (free trade publication)
    2500 Tamiami Trail N.
    Nokomis, FL 34275
    941-966-9521; fax 941-966-2590
    www.comnews.com

Contingency Planning and Management (free trade publication)
    84 Park Avenue
    Flemington, NJ 08822
    908-788-0343; fax 908-788-3782
    www.contingencyplanning.com/index.cfm

Council on Library and Information Resources
Commission on Preservation and Access
    1755 Massachusetts Avenue, N.W., suite 500
    Washington, DC 20036
    202-939-4750; fax 202-939-4765
    www.clir.org

Disaster Recovery Journal (free trade publication)
    Box 510110
    St. Louis, MO 63151
    314-894-0276; fax 314-894-7474
    www.drj.com

Enterprise Systems Journal (free trade publication)
    c/o Cardinal Business Media, Inc.
    P.O. Box 2061
    Skokie, IL 60076-7961
    866-293-3194; fax 847-647-9295
    www.esj.com

Records Management Quarterly
    Association of Records Management and
        Administrators, Inc.
    4200 Somerset, suite 215

    Prairie Village, KS 66208-5287
    800-422-2762 (U.S. and Canada);
        fax 913-341-3742
    www.arma.org/index.cfm

Survive International: The Business Continuity Group (free trade publication)
    First Floor, Waterman House
    101-107 Chertsey Road
    Woking, Surrey GU21 5BW
    United Kingdom
    +44 1483 710600; fax +44 1483 710601
    1-800-SURVIVE; fax 212-371-8325
    www.survive.com

Internet Addresses and Websites

American Fire Sprinkler Association (AFSA)—
automatic fire sprinklers
    afsainfo@firesprinkler.org
    www.sprinklernet.org
    www.sprinklernet.org/sprinklerinfo/index.html

CoOL: Conservation On-Line
    palimpsest.stanford.edu

Federal Emergency Management Agency (FEMA)
    www.fema.gov

Florence 30 years after the flood (pictures, photos, and stories of the conservation efforts during the flood and afterward)
    www.mega.it/allu/eng/ealluvho.htm

National Association of Fire Equipment Distributors (selection and design of alarm and suppression systems)
    401 North Wabash Avenue, suite 732
    Chicago, IL 60611
    312-245-9300; fax 312-245-9301
    www.nafed.org

National Fire Protection Association
    P.O. Box 9101
    1 Batterymarch Park
    Quincy, MA 02269-9101
    617-770-3000; fax 617-770-0700
    www.nfpa.org/Home/index.asp

Index

Miriam Kahn has specialized in preservation and disaster response since 1989. Her company, MBK Consulting, was founded in 1991 and provides preservation and disaster response services to all types of cultural institutions, corporations, and small to medium-sized businesses and disaster response companies. Kahn received her MLS from Queens College, CUNY and worked as preservation officer for the State Library of Ohio, coordinator for online services at the I. D. Weeks Library at the University of South Dakota, and reference librarian at New York Public Library—Mid Manhattan Branch. In addition to her consulting business, she teaches workshops and seminars for librarians and archivists on a wide variety of topics including preservation and disaster response.